ALL IN

ALL IN

HOW GREAT LEADERS BUILD

UNSTOPPABLE TEAMS

Mike Michalowicz

Portfolio | Penguin

PORTFOLIO / PENGUIN
An imprint of Penguin Random House LLC
penguinrandomhouse.com

Most Portfolio books are available at a discount when purchased in quantity
for sales promotions or corporate use. Special editions, which include personalized
covers, excerpts, and corporate imprints, can be created when purchased in
large quantities. For more information, please call (212) 572-2232 or e-mail
specialmarkets@penguinrandomhouse.com. Your local bookstore can also assist
with discounted bulk purchases using the Penguin Random House corporate
Business-to-Business program. For assistance in locating a participating retailer,
e-mail B2B@penguinrandomhouse.com.

LIBRARY OF CONGRESS CATALOGING-IN-PUBLICATION DATA
Names: Michalowicz, Mike, author.
Title: All in : how great leaders build unstoppable teams / Mike Michalowicz.
Description: New York : Portfolio/Penguin, [2024] |
Includes bibliographical references and index.
Identifiers: LCCN 2023015161 (print) | LCCN 2023015162 (ebook) |
ISBN 9780593544501 (hardcover) | ISBN 9780593544518 (ebook)
Subjects: LCSH: Teams in the workplace. | Leadership.
Classification: LCC HD66 .M53 2024 (print) | LCC HD66 (ebook) |
DDC 658.4/022—dc23/eng/20230407
LC record available at https://lccn.loc.gov/2023015161
LC ebook record available at https://lccn.loc.gov/2023015162

Printed in the United States of America
1st Printing

Book design by Alissa Rose Theodor

Dedicated to Helen Fuller,
because that's what Dad would have wanted.

CONTENTS

INTRODUCTION

As first days go, Alexander Vasiliev's was among the very worst. By the end of his shift working as a security guard at the Boris Yeltsin Presidential Center in Yekaterinburg, Russia, he had cost his employer more than $3,000, faced criminal charges, and made the international news—and all it took to wreak so much havoc was a pen. Bored, Vasiliev drew two pairs of eyes on the blank faces in Anna Leporskaya's avant-garde masterpiece *Three Figures*. The painting was valued at nearly $1 million and on loan from the State Tretyakov Gallery in Moscow. Vasiliev was fired, along with the security firm, and they ended up paying for the painting's restoration. When asked about his little doodle, er, act of vandalism, Vasiliev said he didn't know the paintings were valuable, he didn't like them, and, oh yeah, some schoolgirls egged him on to draw on the faces. Sure, dude.

More than five thousand miles away, Ben Bjork, a security guard at the Baltimore Museum of Art, had a very different job experience.

For years, he'd stared at *50 Dozen* by artist Jeremy Alden, a chair made out of six hundred No. 2 pencils. Bjork had fantasized about sitting in the chair, but he never made a move to do so, because he knew he couldn't. He and his fellow guards had a deep respect for the art.

Then museum board member Amy Elias came up with the idea to invite the guards to curate their own exhibition, "Guarding the Art." Over the yearslong preparation, the security sentinels made all the decisions about the show, from which pieces would be on display to the color of the paint on the walls. As they gained a better understanding of the process, they learned about the need for art to work harmoniously and fluidly; they also came to better understand their role at the museum. Now they have a different view of their relationship to the art.

Traci Archable-Frederick, a security guard who chose the contemporary collage piece *Resist #2* by Mickalene Thomas, said, "I'm very proud of this piece, as if it I did it myself." As for Bjork, he chose the chair he'd been thinking about for so long. He had always protected the piece, and now he wanted to celebrate it. In his label copy, he stated: "I chose *50 Dozen* in part because it's funny for me to think of a chair that would break if you actually sat on it, like it's a prank on the tired guards."

As business leaders, we search high and low for employees who give more, do more, and want more, like the security guards at the Baltimore Museum of Art, and yet we more commonly end up with people who take a Sharpie to our priceless masterpiece—if we can find any candidates at all. And because we don't have a solid team, we spend way too much time and money trying to find better people and keep the employees we *do* have. If we're lucky, we have a couple awesome people on staff, yet their work is compromised because their coworkers don't pull their weight.

Throw in disruption—a global health emergency, generational divide, shifting work standards and policies—and staffing your company, much less building a team that rocks it every day, is a relentless struggle. It seems as though most days are like managing unruly adolescents, and as soon as you get a handle on them, someone mucks it all up again for the team. All this volatility is hard enough on corporations; for small businesses, it can be devastating.

Since I wrote my first book in 2008, I have devoted myself to helping entrepreneurs like me, the people who started their businesses and ran them. Then the call came from one of those megacorporations: Guardian Insurance. Maria Ferrante-Schepis was tasked with figuring out how to build a sales team who adored their clients, cared for the company, and were all in on their job. Yes, Guardian had done years of research and found some interesting stuff. But it was big corporate stuff. What this HR leader wanted was the secret that successful small businesses—like mine, and those of so many entrepreneurs I had gotten to know—had figured out. Huh. A big company wants to know how *we* do it? At first I was surprised, but then I realized their interest made sense.

Small businesses don't offer employees huge ladders to climb. The work is not steady. Micro-enterprises can rarely win a compensation offer battle. And we can't hide hiring mistakes with "fill-in-the-blank" positions. We are underfunded and underresourced, and yet many entrepreneurs pull it off. Some small companies are stacked with "A-players," yet the reason why is not so obvious.

I thought about my colleagues and other small-business owners who have remarkable, loyal, and motivated teams. They don't have employees who kill time until they can clock out or do the bare minimum until they can find a "better" job. They have rock-star employees who can do the job they were hired to do, who love their work, and who seek ways to contribute and solve problems. Employees who are all in, who care as much about the companies they work for as the owners do.

Stop for a moment and consider that possibility. What could you do if you had a team that cared as much about your company—its mission, customers, growth, *future*—as you do? The truth is, it's not a pipe dream. It's a necessity. You can't drive profitability, manage disruption, or scale your company if your team doesn't care about your business.

When I scratched out my first business plan at the tender-and-clueless age of twenty-three, I couldn't have imagined a team like that. Heck, I didn't even know I needed one. I figured I'd hire people who were qualified to do the work, they'd show up, and we'd all do our best to deliver good service to our customers. Wrong! Cue the annoying game show buzzer. To find and keep great employees, I tried all the (wrong) things, and then more (wrong) things, and then I invented some wacky things and tried them too. But I kept coming back to the same challenges. Regardless of my efforts, I felt paralyzed, disheartened, and helpless. Recruiting people, retaining people, let alone "raising the bar," was a constant life of frustration and feeling overwhelmed.

Having a team that cares as much about our company as we do seems unobtainable, doesn't it? And it sounds like a myth, as difficult as finding the Holy Grail. The great news is, it's not.

I used to believe that 10 percent of the population (or some other small rando number) were great workers and everyone else sucked. That all the good people were already employed, and that anyone seeking a job wasn't employed because they weren't employable. I thought I was an A-player and no one else could measure up.

After years of struggling to build a team that could not only handle the work but could help grow my company, I started to think differently about my role in that struggle. I had always thought of myself as an entrepreneur. I applied business strategy to get more top clients, to achieve and maintain profitability, to refine my business so that it would run without me, and to market my business in a way that got my ideal prospects' attention. And yet when I tried to apply "business strategy" to team building, it would always crumble. I tried to build a better team by building a better business, when in reality I needed to become a better leader. Not just a decent leader, or even a good leader. A *great* leader.

If I wanted my employees to be all in, I needed to be all in on my employees. Let me repeat that with a slight rephrase, since repetition is the mother of mastery:

If *you* want *your* employees to be all in, *you* need to be all in on *your* employees.

And that's what I did. I went all in. More specifically, I learned how to go all in and then practiced it. I figured out that everyone feels like an A-player—me, you, all of us. And the truth I discovered is we are *all* A-players. Yes, everyone is an A-player. Some are just A-players in waiting. That's called potential.

Through trial, error, and a whole lot of humble pie, I identified a formula that would create the right conditions to find and nurture that potential. I trusted the process, stuck with it, and now I have a team packed with top performers. Business leaders now come to take a tour of our tiny, eight-person office, meet the team, and see how we do it. And the thing is, we just do the best of what you don't see at most other companies. We took ideas from sports teams, universities, religious practices, and, most important, psychological/behavioral research. And voilà, our team is curating art—not a single Sharpie face in the place.

I made it my mission to study the companies that had figured out how to build remarkable teams. In my research, and in interviewing, arguably interrogating, business leaders who did it right, I hoped to find the missing link, the one key difference they all applied to their organizations. Instead, I found four. And those four strategies became a leadership formula I applied to my own companies. And it worked.

I have tried to learn from great leaders, and I have implemented their ideas—sometimes clumsily. I am far from perfect, but I have found that even implementing bits and pieces has had a significant positive impact on our company. Our team continues to surprise and delight me as we work together to grow our organization.

You don't have to amplify your leadership abilities by 100 percent tomorrow—or ever. You don't have to be perfect as you try to implement new ideas. And you don't need to do all that you learn here. All that matters is you get started and commit to continuous improvement.

You can lead an extraordinary team that is all in for your company. In fact, it will happen because you are all in for them.

ALL IN

1

Why Most Teams Just Don't Care

There's busted. And then there's *busted*.

On paper, Elliott seemed like the one. We needed a solid computer tech and he seemed to have all the right credentials. He was proficient in the right hardware and software. He had years of experience doing the same thing we did. I didn't notice one single typo on his résumé, a clear demonstration of his attention to detail. And a bonus—he was fluent in Spanish!

His interview went well. He was articulate and likable. His suit fit and his tie complemented his shirt, which is a small miracle for a computer guy. Even though I had only met with three candidates at that point, I hired him on the spot. It wasn't that I had necessarily hit the jackpot with Elliott. I chose not to interview anyone else because he checked all our boxes—and I was already overwhelmed. Wasting time interviewing more folks would be costly and draining. I needed someone pronto, as in yesterday.

My business partner and I couldn't handle the workload anymore. We had started our company, Olmec Systems, to provide tech support to local businesses, and as we grew, we both kept doing the client work we'd always done. By the time we posted the job announcement for a tech, we were beyond exhausted. We felt paralyzed and helpless. Helpless to find the help we needed. Isn't that frustrating? When you need help the most, you have the least amount of time and energy to make it happen.

Those days, I dragged myself home from work, long after my kids went to bed, and then got up early to do it all over again. Every Monday I told myself, *If I can just get past this week, I'll have the time to find and develop the right person.* But it never happened.

We needed our clones, or as close to clones as we could get. Someone who had a pulse, could type at a keyboard and plug in a few wires. The other two candidates we interviewed were questionable on the pulse part. So a guy with the experience we were looking for, who wore a fitted suit and had a résumé on heavy-stock paper, was nothing short of a godsend.

On his first day on the job, I immediately sent Elliott out into the field to support our clients—with no substantial training. Clearing my throat here—when I say he received "no substantial training," I really mean he got none. Squat. Zilch-ola. No meeting. No "get to know you" chat. No there's the bathroom, there's your desk, feel free to walk around. When Elliott showed up on the morning of day one, I gave him the addresses of clients to visit, problems to fix, and pushed him out the door—literally.

We had clients who urgently needed services that day, and when Elliott turned back to ask, "What should I . . . ?" I put my hand on his shoulder as if to say, "You've got this," and gave him a gentle shove (aka, a hard-ish push) out the door. As he walked toward his car carrying the tech tool kit I gave him, I cried out after him, "Call me if you need me."

Yeah, sending him right out into the field was another hasty move, but I didn't have the time to train him. We needed him to pay for himself starting from day one. Plus, that's how I started my first job. Trial by fire! On-the-job learning! If it's on your résumé, you can do it.

Within hours, Elliott started calling with questions. "How do I do this?" and "How do I configure that?" and "Why won't this thing work with that thing?" And my favorite question (as in my least favorite of all time): "Hey, this client only speaks Spanish. How do I ask them where the bathroom is?" Didn't the résumé specify he was fluent in Span . . . ugh, forget it.

The person we hired to help us manage our client load couldn't handle anything on his own. Instead of freeing up our time, he put more of a burden on me and my partner. I couldn't do the tech work I needed to do when I was talking Elliott through his. But wasted time was the least of our problems. He quickly formed the infamous reverse "golden handcuffs."

As he became familiar with our clients and their systems, Elliott started to learn elements of their technology that only he could support. He set up computers his own way, not ours. I wasn't aware of how he configured certain technology and (sinfully) didn't know some of the passwords he set. Within a month, Elliott didn't feel that he had to stay with our company; I felt I needed him to stay.

Elliott had tied my hands behind my back and the handcuffs were locked. He had the golden key. I was at his whim. If one of our clients had a problem, I was required to have Elliott do the work. Talk about leverage. I couldn't fire Elliott, he could "fire" me, the leader, and leave me in the lurch trying to figure out how he supported our clients.

Even though he seemed incapable of doing much of the work and uninterested in taking direction from me, his boss, he had become indispensable. He knew stuff I didn't, so firing him would screw up client relationships and exhaust me further. I was frozen in frustration.

Then Elliott said, "We need to talk compensation. People at my level get paid double what I make. I feel I'm getting shortchanged, Mike. I don't feel good about that and suspect you don't either. I hope you will fix that for me before I'm needed to save a client from a network disaster." OMG. Seriously? Was my employee shaking me down?

I started to think, *Maybe if I pay him more, he'll be more motivated. He'll listen to me. He'll do better.* That moment introduced me to the weirdest employment vortex I have ever experienced. The exact guy I wanted to fire so badly was the exact guy I was trying to figure out how to pay more. Maybe if I took the few dollars I had been allocating as a salary for myself and gave it to Elliott, it would convince him to stay, and stay happy. (I made $17,000 in my third year of owning a company in 1998. In today's dollars that's *negative* $500.)

It wasn't so much that Elliott was shaking me down. I was shaking myself down. In the hopes of converting him from a bad employee to a good one, I wanted to pay a guy who sucked at his job *more money.* I held on to a not-working-out worker because I was terrified of the hiring process that clearly didn't work. The thought of the effort needed for training and retaining made it worse. And now I planned to forgo the few dollars I took home to pay an employee who had all the power.

Maybe I could work with him to improve his job performance.

Maybe I could come up with a way to motivate him to be more invested in our company's success.

Maybe unicorns would fly down from Mars and sprinkle him with magic "caring" glitter, so he'd suddenly start doting on our clients instead of on himself.

In mid-December, about three months into his employment, all my "maybes" were answered with a clear "F no." Elliott left a voicemail for me with some sad news. "My grandmother passed away yesterday, unexpectedly. My family and I are devastated. I have to go to Georgia for her funeral this Friday. I will be gone for a week."

Elliott seemed dismayed about losing his grandmother, and yet something seemed fishy. First, his voice sounded funny, as though he had cupped his hand over the receiver to block out surrounding party noise. And he left me the muffled message at 1 a.m. on a Saturday. And, *and*, I could hear the infectious beat of "Jump" by Kris Kross cranking in the background. Not the typical mournful music played when a loved one passes. We all grieve in our own way, but with wiggida wiggida wack hip-hop?

Despite my apprehension, I would never deny an employee time off to go to a funeral, so I left him a return message offering my condolences and gave him a week off—paid, of course. Then I immediately went to work covering our clients, with one-third of our staff out of commission.

That's when the Bahama Mama hit the fan.

About midweek, one of our clients left me a voicemail. "Oh my gosh. You're the best boss ever," he said. "I ran into Elliott in the Bahamas. It's so amazing that you gave him a week off to be at The Buzz 99.3 FM party."

Say what now?

Elliott had been kicking it at some sort of weeklong party on a Caribbean island while we picked up his slack—and paid for his vacation?

And wait. Just. One. Second. He *might* not be partying the blues away. *Maaaaaybeeeee* his grandma's death was a story. As in the made-up kind.

I started my business as an entrepreneur, but after hiring my first employee I was now a career sleuth in training. Since I wasn't 100 percent sure our client had the right guy, I sent a bouquet of lilies to Elliott's parents with a note that read "I'm so sorry about the passing of your mother. Elliott told me how much she meant to your family."

That's when everything blew up. Confused by the note, Elliott's parents called him, and us. Grandma was alive and well after all. (I'll bet you figured that out way before I did.) Turns out Elliott had won a contest on the radio for a party in the Bahamas that prior Saturday (I assume around 1 a.m., but what do I know?), and he'd used his meemaw as an excuse to get paid time off.

Elliott was *busted*. Not just regular busted. You-fake-killed-off-your-grandma type of busted.

His parents were furious (I hope). I was furious (for sure). And Elliott? He was out of a job. (Most definitely.)

If he had just come to me and said he won the tickets, I would have accommodated him. I would have said, "A weeklong party on an island, for free? Heck yeah! Go forth! Remember to hydrate." Instead, he defaulted to manipulation to get his way. Which I only later realized was his modus operandi.

The fallout after firing Elliott was tough. I had to explain to the clients he served why he had been let go, and then fix all the problems and inconsistencies he'd created. After four months, we were right back where we started—exhausted and doing all the work. Actually, it was worse. We lost trust with some of our clients. Elliott had left their systems in a lurch, and we didn't even have the @#$%@!

passwords. We didn't hire an employee who was all in and now we had a handful of clients who were all gone.

According to Trakstar, "bad hires" cost companies thousands of dollars, but you didn't need anyone to tell you that. You might be surprised to learn that according to a Harris Interactive Poll, 41 percent of business owners said bad hires cost them more than $25,000. I hope that *is* a surprise to you. And I surely hope you are not thinking, "I wish it was *only* $25K." Beyond the recruitment and hiring expense, there's the cost of unproductive time, unhappy or lost clients, disruption to others. When an employee doesn't fit, it can undermine morale and the performance of the entire team. And the bossy boss, you, loses sleep as a bonus.

Long after I fired Elliott, I kept frothing about the locked accounts, the fake-dead grandma, all that stuff. I ranted to anyone who would listen to me. When I caught a glimpse of myself in the mirror after a particularly animated diatribe, my face red and spittle at the corners of my mouth, I made a solemn pledge: *No more bad hires.*

THE EMPLOYEE ENGAGEMENT DARTBOARD

Over time, I learned how to hire more patiently. And I found some good people who really cared. But I still struggled to keep all my employees engaged, and to build a team where everyone cared as much as I did.

Five years later, I sold my interest in Olmec in a private equity deal and went on to cofound a computer forensic investigation business. As I grew as a leader, I knew the essence of a successful company was an extraordinary team. I'm convinced you know the same. But knowing and doing are two different things. And as much as I wanted an unstoppable team packed with rock-star employees, I struggled.

I now consider my second company a Petri dish for team building. It was as if I was tossing darts at a "strategies for employee engagement" dartboard and trying whichever one my mini arrow hit. And when it didn't work as well as I hoped, or not at all, I picked up my darts and gave it another go. I tried paying more money and increasing benefits. I tried shorter workdays and flex time. Longer workdays with shorter workweeks. I tried creating a company culture and set of corporate values. I put motivational quotes on the walls. I tried team-building exercises and employee recognition. I tried rallying my troops around one big goal—and around defeating one common enemy. I even tried bringing in the cheesy foosball table.

Some of the strategies I tried "worked," but they were only temporary solutions. And even when I had one or two superstar employees, the rest of the team seemed disengaged. I wanted an entire team of performers. I wanted a team that cared as much as I did, and I started to believe it wasn't possible. After all, I'm an entrepreneur. I built the business. I am the shareholder. I reap the rewards when we win: the money goes to me, the accolades go to me, the ego is all mine. Who is going to care about the business as much as me?

IT'S NOT YOU, IT'S ME

We were in the right place at the right time. Our forensics company became an industry authority, but the engine fueling that company—my team—was fragile. We had three rock-star employees and the other folks all seemed to fall a bit short here and there. Just when we started to fracture, we sold the company to Robert Half International.

Unlike my last exit, this time I would stay on with the company for a year. I had no clue what was expected of me or what my role was. Simply that I was to do—something.

Now I wasn't the boss. I was the employee.

The first official day of the acquisition I reported to our existing building as instructed. No one from Robert Half was there. No one contacted us. No one called. No one stopped by. No one acknowledged our existence. I was pushed out the door of my old business and into the job at a new one, with the expectation to get stuff done. But I had no clue what to do. The only thing I got was an email from the new boss saying, "Call me if you need anything." Just one cryptic email. No instructions. No training. No nothing.

A few hours later, I called in to the main office to try to figure out what to do (my new "boss" neglected to include his number in his email). I got hold of no one. Crickets. Everyone remembers their first day of work, and mine was the deafening sound of silence.

That evening, my wife, Krista, asked, "How'd your first day go, Mr. Corporate Guy?" She was excited that I was finally off the entrepreneurial hamster wheel and had a "real" and "reliable" job.

"I don't know," I said. "Like, I just sat there. I didn't know what to do and no one directed me. No one even talked to me. If I had to put my feeling of today in one word, it would be *abandoned*."

Abandoned. It was my first day, and I felt discarded by the company I intended to devote myself to. I started that first day at 8 a.m. ready to roll, and by the time I was talking with my wife at 8 p.m. that night, I was ready to resign. Twelve measly hours.

Within a few weeks, Robert Half started shifting some of the former team into different roles—roles that didn't make sense. For example, they moved Maryellen, who managed forensic investigations, to a (much) lesser position: data entry. They never interviewed her; they never asked about her; they just said, "This is what you do now." Her job was to fill in the blank.

Maryellen started coming in to work with tears pouring down her face. "I hate it here," she'd say. "They're destroying me. I don't know what to do. I need a job, but I can't do this."

I wanted to help Maryellen and the others who suddenly found themselves stuck in roles that didn't make sense or were following protocols they didn't understand. The boss at Robert Half shuffled our people around to fill in the next open spot. And me? I had no authority. I was just told to work.

My new boss, John (or was it Frank, or Ken?), gave me zero direction, except a billable-hours metric that I couldn't fulfill because I *had no direction*. With no communication, no guidance, and no sense of control, I quickly disconnected from the business, and from my former team. No one talked about "quiet quitting" at that time, but that term fits how I felt—and behaved. Robert Half went through twelve months of due diligence to acquire our company, and within twelve hours they had lost my heart.

Mistakes were made. Project conflicts became the norm. And my formerly thriving business started to collapse. Projected to do $7 million the year we were acquired, we pulled in a dismal $300,000. This is when leadership at Robert Half started to freak out.

John called me into his office. "Mike," he said, "we need you to fix this. We now understand from your team that you oversaw the operations. You're in the wrong position here. You really should be a director."

I scoffed. I'm not proud of it, but I did. I had owned a sizable portion of the company they just acquired, and yet they had never interviewed me about what I do, so they had no idea I handled the day-to-day operations. Now that everything was screwed up, they wanted me to step in and fix it.

I declined the offer and went back to my "job," which I deemed should now include speaking to aspiring entrepreneurs about building and selling companies, and the pitfalls that can ensue.

Months later, I was fired.

John called me to the conference room this time. The ominous one, right next to the HR office. There he sat at the head of the table, with the HR person to his right and someone whom I presume was another one of my "bosses" at his left. Corporate rule #1: Cover your ass. One firing = two witnesses.

John is a good person. You could just feel that about him. But the stress of the corporate machine was crushing him too. So his emotions got the better of him, and he screamed. His face went beet red. He yelled at me and my failure to deliver for the company. He cursed and pointed at me. "Why don't you do anything? How can you bring so many credentials and be so useless? How come you are speaking to aspiring entrepreneurs on the company's dime?"

The veins on his temple pulsed with uncontrollable anger. He was a man at his wit's end. And yet all I could think was, *This guy's a dick.*

I stared at the spittle forming at the corner of his frothing mouth, and I remembered my own steaming-mad red face in the mirror after one of my Bahama Elliott rants. Right then, the truth slapped me in the face:

John isn't a dick. Nor is Elliott.

I am.

I am the dick.

And now *I* was busted.

All these years, I thought Elliott was the problem, when it was really my lack of leadership. I barely interviewed him. I never trained him. I threw him into the field without so much as a welcome lunch, let alone a potty break. I avoided his calls on day one, and two, and every day after.

I never got to know him, I didn't make time to listen to his ideas, and I didn't create a work environment where he felt comfortable sharing awesome news, like winning an awesome trip. I never considered his potential nor tried to develop it. I expected him to serve my company and could care less about serving him. I treated him like a resource, like a friggin' human resource, not a human being.

Would Elliott have worked out had I done all those things right? Maybe. Maybe not. But I could no longer deny my part in the problem.

On Elliott's first day home from working with me, a loved one surely asked him, "How was your first day?" And I can only suspect he responded like I did on my first day. "Meh" at best. "Abandoned" at worst.

Now, on the other side of poor leadership, I realized that if I wanted a top-performing team, I was the one who needed to change. I needed to learn the tools of great leadership.

As I walked out through the revolving door onto the sidewalk of Avenue of the Americas in New York City, I felt extraordinary relief and enlightenment. Right then and there, I knew I would start a new company with a new *me*, and it felt so good. And this time would be different. In that moment, I vowed to become the greatest leader I could be. To lead a team of employees who loved coming to work, who were strengthened and energized by their job, and who felt encouraged to be themselves and contribute to the company in their own unique ways because they knew their leaders deeply cared for them. From that day forward, I would go all in for my team. And this time, I would have an entire team that would go all in for the company.

WHAT DOES IT REALLY MEAN TO BE ALL IN?

You may be thinking, "Mike, I *do* care about my employees. I *am* all in for them." I know you care, or you wouldn't have picked up this book. The challenge for us as leaders is that we have a different perspective about work, and our company, than do our employees. And until we understand this fundamental difference, no amount of caring will create the team we want.

According to the Pew Research Center, more than half the people who work for a private company say that their job is simply what they do for a living. Yet nearly two-thirds of business owners and leaders say their job gives them an identity. This is a massive gap.

I have a theory about why the gap is so big. Think about it—as a business leader, you have unlimited potential and possibilities. You can follow your desires. You can become the person you want to be because *you* are in control. I know it may not feel that way when you're working your ass off on a Saturday, or when you seem to be at the mercy of your deadlines, or your customers, or society. Despite how you may feel, you have more control over your future at your company than your team has over theirs. You have potential that you can live into. Your work allows you to explore and express your true identity.

Identity. That's the gap. The bridge between you and your team is identity. Specifically, the bridge is empowering people to explore and express their true identity. To support them, guide them, help them in expressing their potential, and, as a result, live into their truest self—their identity.

To be all in for your employees is to recognize and nurture their potential, to set the stage for your team to tap into their biggest desires and empower them to express their real selves. I believe my role is to help everyone on my team become more of who they are, who they feel called to be. When you adopt this belief as your own, you can more easily create the conditions you need to build your all-in team. If you don't make this shift, the formula I'm about to share with you won't work as well as it could. It just won't.

Bronnie Ware, author of *The Top Five Regrets of the Dying*, who herself experienced years of unfulfilling work, started a process while working in palliative care. She asked her dying patients to share their biggest regrets. Number one? "I wish I'd had the courage to live a life true to myself, not the life others expected of me." True to myself. That is the friggin' definition of identity. People want to live their identity. They want to explore and develop their potential. People want to be the most of who they can be.

And there you have it. A great leader empowers people to be themselves fully. When you do that earnestly and perpetually, your team will blossom. Your people will blossom. And you too will blossom.

THE ALL-IN FORMULA

There is no magic wand for the recruiting process.

A fancy interview question such as "When should you speed through a yellow light versus stop for one?" tells you nothing about a candidate. Asking A-players to introduce their A-player friends rarely yields much. And while a résumé packed with loads of applicable experience may give you a bit more than nothing, it is potentially the most dangerous misleader in the world of recruiting and retention.

Sometimes we try to fix our staffing issues by making "one key shift," but humans don't work like that. No single question brings in the best and filters out the rest. Your existing team won't turn on like a lightbulb; they won't suddenly become the employees you dream about simply by your introducing motivating values.

To flourish, we need the right set of conditions, created by great leaders. Over time, I did assemble a remarkable team. In fact, my team is *beyond* anything I could have dreamt up. What worked for me and for the leaders I have subsequently interviewed and counseled wasn't one strategy that produced better results over another, or one insight that mattered more than the rest. It was a formula that ensured my team cared about my company as much as I did. And it wasn't through coercion and correction, or rewards and recognition. It was through something more fundamental. Something more essential to the way we humans operate. The formula works for the company I lead. It works for the leaders I have consulted. And it will work for you if you embrace it. I am sure of it, because it is the most empowering way to help people be themselves. Their true selves.

The All-In Formula has four parts, and it breaks down like this:

fit + ability + safety + ownership = all-in team

I call it the FASO Model. I simply pronounce it "faso." As in rhyming with the word "lasso." Let's get this rodeo started, shall we?

Fit. A company is a congregation of people and tools that work in concert to achieve specific outcomes. People will come, grow, and go. People aren't the constant in a company, nor should they be; the roles are. To ensure your employees are a good fit, first understand all the functions of a role, and the qualities and qualifications required for that role. Then enlist people for the position matching their potential, talents, and identity to the role's tasks. Don't look for a person who can do it all; that is a rare situation. Look for the person who is best at what you need most; they are abundantly available.

Ability. Great leaders know people are far more than their résumé. Hiring based on experience and education is limiting—for your team, and for your company's growth. Rather than match a person's qualifications to a role, consider a person's innate, experiential, and potential abilities. People who want to do a job always outperform people who need to do a job. Seek the want. The desire. The thirst.

Safety. People do their best when they are not worried by the rest. Protect your team and set up conditions in which they feel safe, enabling them to lean in to contribution. There are three types of safety to consider: Physical safety, where they have protection from harm to their physical self. Financial safety, where they can maintain their life standard without concern for how they will sustain themselves each day. And psychological safety, where they have confidence that they won't be punished, ridiculed, or humiliated for expressing their true opinions, beliefs, background, or experience.

Ownership. If you want your team to act like owners, make sure they feel like owners. This one insight alone, put into effect, transforms perfunctory performance into all-out effort. Once we have an employee who does the right job for their abilities, who feels safe to be themselves at work, the next critical step is to foster psychological ownership—a sense of control, understanding, and personalization—over a task, project, or idea.

Psychological ownership is the strongest influence over self-identity: What is mine is me and what is me is mine. My ideas are me. My possessions are an extension of me. When team members are designated ownership over aspects of their job, the natural tendency is for them to put everything they have into it.

There you have it. The All-In Formula. F+A+S+O. It can be helpful to think about the formula like this:

Fit and ability (where potential meets opportunity—identity is developed)

Safety and ownership (where development meets environment—identity is expressed)

Each part is effective on its own, but together, these strategies have a multiplicative effect. Deploy the formula properly, and I promise you, you will build the team of your dreams.

FASO will care for you so well that I invite you to make it the primary tool in your leadership tool kit. Like a quality Swiss Army knife or similar multitool, FASO will serve you in circumstances foreseen and not. So memorize it.

I love a good acronym, but I have the tendency to garble things up. When I was a kid, I struggled with memorizing facts, or strings of numbers, or, well, anything. Until someone whispered in my ear a mnemonic.

My seventh-grade music class scared the hell out of me. In chorus the teacher would go down the line and make each student sing a few words a cappella. Sara McMickle, who stood next to me, always nailed her part. As in Celine Dion nailed it. Then I would go and, you know, not nail it. "Again, Michael," the teacher would say. I would feel the heat on my face, and I would sing worse. The teacher would repeat her request, this time in a sing-say melody. Ahhhhh!

The only thing more terror-inducing to me than singing was memorizing the music notes on a sheet. Seemingly random dots, identified by random letters, sat across random lines that started off with a squiggly cliff. Or clef. Or cliff-clef. Ugh. But then Sara whispered something to me. "Every good boy deserves fudge." She pointed at each line on the sheet music clef. E for "every," G for "good," B for "boy," D for "deserves," and F for "fudge." From that moment on, I never forgot it. I still couldn't sing, but you can't have everything.

FACE is a simple way to remember the notes in the empty spaces on the clef. HOMES is a simple mnemonic to remember the Great Lakes—Huron, Ontario, Michigan, Erie, and Superior. And if you want to be an extraordinary leader of extraordinary employees you will greatly benefit from a simple mnemonic too. Try this one: FASO, a Fully Autonomous and Seamless Organization. That's what you want! And FASO will get you there. If you remember it and deploy it, you will become the best damn leader for the best damn team. Damn it.

MY UNSTOPPABLE TEAM

I don't have to work weekends anymore. My punishing schedule is long gone. From time to time, though, I still go in on early Saturday mornings to write or brainstorm. I like the special quiet of an empty office before the world wakes.

One Saturday, I looked up from my notebook to see Amy Cartelli walking in sipping a cup of coffee. She was immediately followed by her husband and both of their sons, all walking in stride. It looked like a 7 a.m. weekend military drill. Three burly men, marching in line, carrying heavy boxes.

"Oh, hey, Mike," said Drill Sergeant Amy. "We're just dropping off books."

"What books? Where did they come from?" I asked.

"These are the copies of *Get Different*. We've been having trouble getting deliveries here at the office, so I redirected the books to my home."

I helped put the boxes away. As I watched Amy and her family leave, I sat stunned. Not only did Amy solve a logistical problem for our company on her own, but she also addressed an issue that I didn't even know about in the first place. She took it upon herself to reroute books and ensure their safe delivery, recruited her family to move the books, and came in on her day off to deliver them. No one asked her to do this. No one expected her to do this. And yet there she was, caring about my company as much as I do.

Over the years, I've experienced many moments like this with my current team—countless examples of how FASO impacts performance—and Amy delivering the books is one of my favorites. You see, she's a part-time employee who only ever wanted to be part-time. And yet even though she doesn't work a full schedule, even though she doesn't need the job, even though she is not locked into her job because of amazing compensation or some other advantage, she *still cares as much about my company as I do.*

What if you had a team full of Amys? What could you do? What goals could you accomplish—for yourself, and for your company? What problems could you solve? What doors would open for you? What projects could you take out of the drawer and try again? What dreams could you realize?

Let's find out.

THE FIRST STEP

I hope you see the potential for being a better leader by approaching team building in a whole new way. Of course, it is unreasonable to expect a transformation overnight. I don't expect you to implement the strategies in this book perfectly, nor do I expect you to dig in tomorrow. I do hope, though, that you'll take the first step today. Then one more tomorrow. And then, eventually, you'll leap.

The first step is easy: Commit to being all in for your team.

I have found that the best way to stick with a new improved you is to first commit. Email me at Mike@MikeMichalowicz.com with the subject line "I'm An All-In Leader" and share a few thoughts with me on how you intend to build your unstoppable team. This is my real email address, and I will get your email. I have an amazing team who help me manage my email, since I am fortunate to have hundreds of reader emails in my inbox at any given moment. My teammates review and summarize the emails and get my direction on the response. So, yes, I will get back to you. I will surely have a colleague press the send button or type what I dictate, but you can be sure my response is my words to you.

2

Eliminate Entropy

Teams are temporary, positions are permanent. No one stays in a job forever, not even you. Yes, occasionally a person will stay with one company for their entire adult life. (Shout-out to my old man, who did just that.) But does that person stay in the same job the entire time? Might they work with different people and do different things during their years or decades of work? Might they retire one day? Inevitably people come and go. So you first need to understand the positions the company needs to grow healthily, and then fulfill those permanent positions with the best, nonpermanent talent. Not the other way around.

Recruiting magic happens when we understand all the parts a position needs first and then seek the individuals (emphasis on the plural) who can fulfill those needs. And yet we tend to focus primarily on finding the right person for a job *title* before we have clarity about which tasks are the most important within that title. We think, "I need a receptionist," and we may have a list of fifteen duties we want that person to perform, but are all their duties necessary for *this* person or even this role? And which tasks are the most important? What if the title was broken into its task elements and an individual's best abilities were matched to those elements? What if they just nailed three critical duties and the other stuff could be assigned to others?

On my desk is a pile of family photos, books I've read, paper notes scatter-stacked, two "dried" (aka dead) plants, and other stuff I haven't found a home for yet. When I first set up my desk, everything had its proper space. It was organized and presentable. But then bits and pieces started to pile up. Now I'm not even sure what color my desk is. Heaven knows what hides away under the piles. This gradual decline into disorder, known as entropy, is a constant in life.

Your organizational entropy is a constant too. Blame it on variables. Take a nickel, for example. It has two sides. Flip it in the air, and you will predictably get either heads or tails. Of course, there is a third option—it could land on its edge. Experiments and simulations confirm this happens once in every six thousand or so attempts. Now take one hundred coins and flip them all in the air at the same time. What are the chances all the coins will land on their edge? Zero—or at least the chances are so close to zero that you will never see this happen. Sure, there is some remote mathematical possibility, just as there's a remote chance your home was built on top of an ancient cemetery and the poltergeists are toying with you before they take possession of your soul, but let's be real: it will never play out that way in reality. Some nickels will be heads up, some tails up, some will roll away under your couch to be swallowed by the demons hiding there. The hundred coins won't line up, they will scatter. Disarray is natural. Entropy is expected.

Entropy is a constant in teams too. As a business evolves, more tasks need completion, more projects need overseeing, things change, and soon you have a mess of "stuff," duties and responsibilities that need to be dusted off and reorganized. In the early days of growing a business, most employees do all sorts of jobs they wouldn't normally do. And as we grow, we promote people, hire new people, move other people into different roles, and can even lose track of the main objective of their job.

A position may have a list of responsibilities with a bunch of tasks on it that were inherited from the person who had the job before them, and nobody remembers why they took on that task in the first place—or even if the task is needed at all. Sometimes the list includes to-dos that were supposed to be temporary and became permanent for no good reason. And then we have the stuff an employee takes on because someone left the company or morphed into a different role, and "someone" had to take over aspects of that person's job. Welcome to organizational entropy.

Once you appreciate that disorder is the normal and natural tendency of all teams, you can apply strategies to prevent it. Just as you can clean a messy desk, or position nickels to stand on their edge, you can align your team. And to do this most effectively, you must reduce variability. We achieve this by setting fewer rules with bigger importance and setting fewer objectives with bigger impact.

Organization takes effort. This is just a fact. Without it, entropy will win. But you can apply effort smartly. When you are clear on the outcome, you blaze the clearest path to it and take down as many barriers as possible. *Your* job is to clear up the confusion, the unnecessary stuff. Your job is to bring priority and organization for your team and with your team. Your job is to fight organizational entropy and to empower them to do the same.

Founded in 1894, Gibson is iconic in the guitar industry. But icons are susceptible to the degrading effects of entropy too. By the 1960s the brand had been rolled up by a conglomerate and within a decade of that was on the verge of closure. Then CEO Henry E. Juszkiewicz leaned in to the natural entropy by expanding the product licenses, creating new instruments, and reviving old product lines. This strategy backfired because consumers were confused by the sheer number of products and configurations. In 2018, Gibson filed for Chapter 11 bankruptcy.

When James "JC" Curleigh took over as CEO, his number one objective was to stop the entropy. He set out to make far fewer guitars, far better. He set fewer, more important rules. One was "no more dust." Literal dust, because when a guitar gets it in the final laminate, it destroys the look. Another simple rule: touch the guitars fewer times, since every time they are handled, the chances for damage increase. He figured out what was needed first, and then asked who can fill that need.

Great leaders don't start by recruiting the best people for the role. Instead, they determine what functions are most important and then find—and keep—the best people to perform those functions. Organizational clarity happens by setting objectives and expectations first, then the match is made with existing or new team members.

THE MUST-HAVE LISTS

The risk leaders run—and it is human nature—is to prioritize every-thing equally. Everything is important. All customers are always right. All tasks must get done. Do it all, do it all perfectly. But the reality is only a few things have big impact, and many other things are of low value.

Part of being all in for our employees is taking the time to get clear about the main function of their role and then paving the way for them to execute that job. Within their grab bag list of responsibilities is the most crucial job within that role, in terms of their regular activity. It is called the Primary Job, which I explain in detail in my book *Clockwork*. This is the core work within the field of responsibility for an employee that they must complete to serve the company, and everything else on the list is secondary to the Primary Job.

You can run a simple exercise to find the Primary Job for anyone. Since I just shared a story about Gibson, I checked for their current job opportunities at this writing. One is a full-time position at their Bozeman, Montana, factory for the afternoon shift. The job lists multiple "essential functions," such as: execute standard operating procedures, maintain an appropriate flow rate, and the use of spring steel blades. Apparently the blades are used to scrape the guitars' non-wooden accents, bringing out the signature aesthetic of a Gibson guitar. And there you have it. Yes, producing fast enough is necessary; drifting from the SOPs (standard operating procedures) and "winging it" is a no-no. But nothing is more important than the scrape. That is the Primary Job and everything else is secondary to it. You can do this for any job listing. And you surely must do it for *your* job listing. Prioritize what matters most.

Before you hire or move employees into different positions, break down what you need for each role—your Must-Have List. The process is simple, and you can knock it out in less than thirty minutes. Here are the steps:

1. For one position in your company, write down every task and responsibility. Include the small stuff, the seasonal stuff, and the stuff you tend to add when you "don't have anyone else to do it."

2. Next, identify the Primary Job. Of all the things on the list, which one thing—and it can only be one—is the most important in moving the company forward? Write "PJ" in the Rank column next to the Primary Job.

3. Now sequence the rest of the list in order of importance.

4. Looking at your ordered list, highlight the "must-haves," the tasks that are absolutely necessary in that position.

5. Everything highlighted is something your employee needs to be able to perform or quickly gain the ability to perform. Anything not highlighted is stuff that "would be nice" for them to be able to do but can wait, can be imperfect, or can be transferred to others.

6. Now that you did it for one, do it for others. Or have others do it for the others.

ROLE: IN-HOUSE COPYWRITER	
RESPONSIBILITY	**RANK**
Editing articles	
Social media copy	
Proofing & grammar checking	
Social media tracking	
Writing articles	
Research	

Figure 1.0

Record each responsibility currently served by
the employee(s) in the defined position.

ROLE: IN-HOUSE COPYWRITER	
RESPONSIBILITY	**RANK**
Editing articles	4
Social media copy	2
Proofing & grammar checking	5
Social media tracking	6
Writing articles	PJ
Research	3

Figure 1.1

Rank the importance of each responsibility in
relation to all listed responsibilities.

ROLE: IN-HOUSE COPYWRITER	
RESPONSIBILITY	**RANK**
Editing articles	4
Social media copy	2
Proofing & grammar checking	5
Social media tracking	6
Writing articles	PJ
Research	3

Figure 1.2

Highlight the minimum "must-have" responsibilities
for the position for any future (or existing) candidates.

When you hire a new employee, or move an employee into a different role, consider if they would be a good fit for the highlighted duties, the must-haves. Don't pay much mind to the rest; those things don't do much to serve the company.

Now that you've carefully defined the duties for each position, consider the type of person who would be the best fit for that role. Think in terms of qualities and qualifications—the 2Qs. For example, let's assume your receptionist's Primary Job is directing inbound support phone calls. The qualities you need for that role are a cheerful attitude, positive energy, a supportive nature, and the ability to be patient under pressure. Qualifications may include previous experience as a receptionist, host, or greeter. You may also want someone who has been trained in customer service, or in a particular phone or software system.

Then do the must-have ranking process. Which qualities are the most critical? Ask yourself, do they *really* need to be meticulous and charming? Or is it meticulous over charming? Or vice versa. And— you know the routine—highlight the absolute "must-haves." Do the same ranking system for qualifications, most important to least, and highlight the must-haves. Does the four-year college degree *really* matter? Does previous experience even matter if they have the highlighted qualities?

The more must-haves you have, the more you are excluding potential candidates. And the fewer you have, the greater the risk that you will be considering candidates who are not a good fit. So use the old handy-dandy 80/20 rule. This is where you derive 80 percent of the benefit from 20 percent of the qualities.

You may be thinking, "Mike, I already *have* a list of qualities and qualifications for each position." I get it. It may seem as though this is a step you can skip because you sense redundancy. First, a reminder—this is a list you create *after* you reduce the variables and clarify the structure of each role. Second, the qualities matter most.

The only thing you can do for new employees is give them skills and experience. You can't give them the intangibles, like their attitude, energy, drive, intelligence, or, for that matter, their heart. Don't hire employees based upon the few things that you can provide them. Hire them based on the many things they naturally do or don't have. I've tried giving intelligence—to myself—and nope, I didn't get smarter. If you can't do it for yourself, good luck doing it for others.

DECONSTRUCTING HIGH PERFORMERS

I've been lucky to have found more than a few high-performing employees. When I discover a true superstar, I have the urge to lock them into their position, because I can't even imagine replacing them. Of course, this is limiting and not realistic. Employees move up and move on, which means you'll eventually have to find someone to take on their role. A common urge is to find their clone. The thing is, what makes these high-performing employees so special is unique to them. The chances that you will find another person "just like them" are somewhere between zero and none.

Leaders often have the same "locked into a person" mentality for multiple roles in their business because, as business grows and changes, we tend to build a position around an individual. When they leave, we call for "all hands on deck," aka panic, to cover the lost talent. Finding someone to replicate the multirole rock star has similar odds: zero to none, minus one.

As you review your must-haves for each role in your organization, consider if you have a position that requires a set of qualities and qualifications that simply cannot be replicated by anyone other than the person currently in that role. If you do, take some time to deconstruct what it is that makes them amazing. Then, if that person moves on from your company or moves up (or over) within your company, you can find people to take on *parts* of their job, not the whole job.

Kelsey Ayres is the best coworker I've ever had the opportunity to work with, the ultimate superstar. She started out working part-time as my personal assistant. Over time, her duties and responsibilities expanded. She is now the president of our company. Her role has evolved over the years, and she's had to give up all the duties she performed as my personal assistant, such as handling my travel schedule for speaking engagements, managing my email, and creating our marketing campaigns.

While I *wanted* to find another person just like Kelsey to fulfill all those duties, I knew that would be harder than finding a needle in a haystack—more like trying to find a single piece of glitter, painted hay color, in a haystack. I also knew her position had evolved over time, and her work responsibilities had entropy maximus. So, we—Kelsey and I—deconstructed the roles she served.

First, we looked at her responsibilities, the looong list of duties she performed not just daily but also weekly, monthly, quarterly, and annually. Then we determined her Primary Job, scheduling my speaking events. We then discussed what the president's Primary Job would likely be. I had been fulfilling that role, and it was management of the rest of the team.

Now, to be clear, I was serving the president role, but I was doing a shitty job at it. I rarely met with people in any organized fashion. Reviews happened when they reminded me another year had passed. Just because I was bad at it doesn't mean it wasn't the Primary Job. Either we had to transfer Kelsey's former Primary Job to someone else or make a new prioritization decision. If Kelsey was going to both manage the people and continue my scheduling, we had to pick which one takes top billing. The goal in this transition was to transfer the management role to Kelsey, and then move scheduling speaking events to someone else.

Then we looked at the other tasks she needed to transfer and identified Kelsey's collective qualities and qualifications. Qualities are innate. But qualifications accumulate. So we noted where she gained her qualifications—on the job here, or prior to joining us—since it might help indicate where the qualifications may come from for the next person.

TASKS SERVED BY: KELSEY					
	QUALITIES		**QUALIFICATIONS**	**FROM**	**TASKS**	**MUST**

	QUALITIES		**QUALIFICATIONS**	**FROM**	**TASKS**	**MUST**
1	Inclusiveness	A	Typing abilities	HAD	One-on-one's	1, 2, 5, 7, B
2	Kindness	B	Fluent in English	HAD	Mike's schedule	2, 3, 6, A, B
3	Accurate research	C	Four-year college degree	HAD	Article writing	3, 8, A, B
4	Fast	D	Past work social work	HAD	Research	3, A, B
5	Emotional intelligence	E	Social media skills	GOT	Article writing	3, 4, A, B
6	Dynamic scheduling	F	US citizen	HAD	Accounting	8, A
7	Listener	G			Writing	7, 8, A, B
8	Meticulous	H			Social media	A, E
9	Frugal	I				
10	Fierce loyalty	J				

Figure 2.0

Deconstruct an existing team member.

STEP 1 ▪ Fill in the name of the person you are deconstructing.

STEP 2 ▪ In the QUALITIES column, list all the positive qualities this person has that supports them in their role.

STEP 3 ▪ In the QUALIFICATIONS column, list all the qualifications this person has that supports them in their role and/or any individual tasks.

STEP 4 ▪ In the FROM column, next to each qualification, write down if the person came to your employ with the qualifications (had) or gained the skills while on the job with you (got).

STEP 5 ▪ In the TASKS column, write down each task this individual does.

STEP 6 ▪ In the MUST column, insert the corresponding number for each quality and corresponding letter for each qualification that is necessary to be successful at the task.

STEP 7 ▪ As you evaluate individuals to fill different tasks, use the TASKS and MUST columns to match the best-suited person for each task.

Next, Kelsey and I played a quick matching game. Of the tasks we were moving to the next person, we identified the qualities and qualifications needed for *each task*. For example, Kelsey is fiercely loyal. She is also frugal. This made her a perfect fit for me because of one of my business Immutable Laws that I refer to as "Blood Money." We treat money like blood, with the utmost care and respect, because without it our business would die. Kelsey's loyalty to the "Blood Money" Immutable Law, combined with her frugality, meant I could always count on her to find the most affordable flights and accommodations for my business travel.

When it came time to transfer the personal assistant duties, we knew we needed to hire someone to do that who was inherently "kind" and "accurate." We went on to define those words. For example, "kind" means to us that we care for and respect people's interests, but it does not mean we are a pushover. We are firm in what we can and can't do, but we aren't a jerk about it. This helped us find the right person for the role, Erin Chazotte, who is both kind and accurate. Plus, she brought a frugality that was like Kelsey's. And she brought a "sternness" that we didn't have before. She expanded on qualities with her own unique talents that made her work within the role even more effective.

Scheduling is not the only responsibility, and there are some other qualities required for other tasks, of course, but in understanding what made Kelsey great at her job we could better find someone to do *parts* of her former job, rather than try to find a Kelsey clone. And you know what happened? We found another superstar in Erin, who is better at scheduling than anyone I worked with before. I believe this is in part due to the work we did "deconstructing" Kelsey. It is also due to the way that Kelsey now leads our company and supports our employees, which you are about to learn.

Erin is such a superstar, in fact, that we are now deconstructing *her* role to find a person to become Kelsey's personal assistant. Will we find another superstar employee? Maybe, maybe not. But with this process, the odds are in our favor.

MATCH TALENT TO TASK

Clint Pulver couldn't sit still. He fidgeted constantly and was deemed an "out of control" kid by his teachers. He would drum his fingers on his desk, on his chair, on any surface he could find. His teachers tried to discipline him, to help him focus. Nothing worked for very long, so the school's principal came up with a genius idea. He told Clint to sit on his hands. Yeah, genius all right.

You can either try to change people to be someone they are not, or you can choose to channel who they already are to the outcomes you—and they—want. Changing myself is near impossible, so why in the world would I ever think I could change someone else? That quality they have, stop trying to block it or correct it and start trying to channel it.

Out of raw frustration, the school put squirming, finger-tapping Clint into a special education class. But the teacher in that room knew the secret to success: Channel behaviors. Don't change them. That teacher, Mr. Jensen, noticed Clint's flying fingers and said, "Oh! You're a drummer." He gave Clint a pair of drumsticks and that was that.

Clint has been playing the drums ever since, and he is *epic*. He played for professional musicians in major venues like the Kodak Theatre in Hollywood, for *America's Got Talent*, and later went on to found the Utah Valley University Drumline and the Green Man Group, which is like the Blue Man Group, but bigger and bad-assier at drums, in my humble opinion.

When an employee doesn't perform in a role the way we expect them to, we tend to think they are not the right fit for our company. It could be, though, that they simply *are* the right person but were inserted into the wrong role.

If you've wondered if an employee will ever measure up, ask yourself, Did you match them with the position that suits them best? Maybe you have an all-in employee waiting to happen, if only you simply recognize their potential and channel who they naturally are. Maybe you have an amazing drummer on your hands, and your job is to stop trying to get them to play guitar better.

Everyone has a strength. I don't think of our employees as employees. I think of them in the same way I think about my family. In my role as a dad, I try to cherish my kids for who they are. Admittedly, this is a discipline. There are times I struggle to "love" my children for their decisions. But the essence is they are human beings whom I have the honor of sharing a life journey with. They, as you and I, should be loved for who they inherently are. I get to know their strengths and weaknesses. I try never to helicopter them, even though at times my heart is screaming to step in and "protect" them. I let them grow, experience the joys and hardships that are a natural part of life, and in all of it hope they achieve full independence, confidence, and love for themselves.

Please don't take this analogy to suggest that you are the parent, and your colleagues are children. That interpretation can result in treating adults like kids. That is not the intent, and it is the opposite of what a great leader does. What I want you to see is that, like a great parent, your job is to give them freedom and support them to grow into who they naturally are. They are part of your family, but they are not your minions.

Once I understand that my job with my colleagues is to support them into the full development of themselves, I am far less about control and more about guiding. I become more fluid in aligning their work experience to amplify their life experience, which in turn amplifies the work experience. The upward spiral makes everyone win: my colleagues, myself, our team, our clients.

As you implement the All-In Formula, you may discover that some of your employees are not in the right roles. And as your company grows and the world evolves, you'll likely have to create new positions. I feel the default is that when the business has the need, we look for someone new. But in reality, when a business has a need, the first ask should be, "What do we do that the business doesn't need?" and then get rid of that. Then ask, "Who here can naturally fill the need we have, and, as a result, do the tasks that play more into who they are?"

Far more people on this planet can quickly fill "entry-level" stuff than "high-level" or "complex" stuff. But your existing people have a leg up. They know the company, and you know them. They may have the skills you need. So seek to reposition people within your company first. Match tasks to talents. Then seek people from the unknown outside to fill the "simpler" or more "entry-level" stuff, and have them develop within your company.

A bit of an asterisk here: You may also know people who are not on your staff but are associated with your company in some capacity. Your familiarity with their qualities and qualifications, and their familiarity with your company, can enable them to get up to speed faster on "senior" stuff. We've hired clients, competitors, subcontractors, and former interns this way, to great success.

THE WHOLE IS GREATER THAN THE INDIVIDUAL

Have you ever seen a barn move across a field, seemingly on its own? If you happened to be on the road adjacent to Joseph Hochstetler's farm in Knox County, Ohio, on March 9, 2019, you might have thought your eyes were playing tricks on you. Looking closer, you would have seen feet underneath the red pole barn—three hundred pairs, to be exact.

Moving a fifty-by-one-hundred-foot multiton structure is a difficult job. You have two options: you can disassemble it and put it back together at the new location, or you can jack it up, use multiple synchronized cranes to place it on custom-designed, synchronized flatbeds with multiple semitruck cabs pulling it, drive it to the new location, and use another group of cranes, in a carefully choreographed move, to lower it onto the new spot. That's all doable, but precarious and hard—unless you're Amish.

Prohibited from using powered tools and machinery, Hochstetler enlisted the help of his three hundred closest friends. From inside the barn, they picked it up in unison and carried it 150 feet across a field, then moved to the outside of the barn and turned it 90 degrees. And they got the job done in less than five minutes.

For the Amish, helping the community is part of their faith. Because everyone rallies when someone is in need, they can often do what seems impossible—build a barn in a day or move one in five minutes. No one says, "That's not my problem." They say, "It's our problem and I am part of the solution." They set aside their own work—their Primary Job—and band together to solve problems and meet challenges. And because they are all committed to the success of the community, they get it done quickly, and then go right back to their Primary Job.

Technology changes our world so rapidly that we face our own "move a barn without power machinery" challenges on the regular. To successfully meet these challenges, we need a nimble team desirous to jump in and help when needed. Rather than say, "That's not my job," we need employees like Hochstetler's pals, people who value community—the good of the whole—above all. Primary Jobs are just that—primary. They are not all the time, eight hours a day. And when we need coordinated, collective help, we need a team that gladly puts all hands in. Or in Hochstetler's case, all hands and feet. (By the way, he didn't respond to my letters asking him to call me for an interview. Apparently he adheres to the Amish rules and doesn't have a phone.)

By eliminating disorder in your team, you make it easier for people to jump in when needed and then get back to their Primary Job.

GOOD AND GREAT LEADERSHIP

Change happens over time. It is rare that someone can instantly re-place one behavior with another. For most of us humans, change is a process of experimentation, proving to ourselves what works and what doesn't. I realize that while you may think some of the ideas in this book could be game changers, or at least worth trying, you may also see some of the ideas in this book as too radical. Or you may think, "That may work for another business, but it won't for mine."

I think skepticism is healthy. And it is also healthy to challenge our established beliefs. But we need to do it in increments. If you try something big once and it fails, that doesn't mean it won't work for your business. It may just mean you need to tailor it to your company or get more practice with it.

Great leaders are willing to challenge their own beliefs. They are willing to prove to themselves, through earnest experimentation and adequate repetition, whether something works or not. In that spirit, I have prepared a list of new approaches I include in *All In*, and the correlating traditional (perhaps old-school) idea that exists.

I suggest that you try the new stuff in small, bite-size pieces and curtail the old stuff in increments. I don't expect everything to work for your leadership style or your corporate community. But I do hope you'll make the effort to discover a better approach, and in the process, a better you.

Good Leaders	Great Leaders
Change Roles Around Employees' Abilities Employees should be lifers and we should do all we can to keep them, as long as they deliver value—including morphing roles to suit them. Good leaders use this approach because it triggers retention. It also restricts individual growth.	**Keep Roles Consistent** Task assignments change over time. To deliver a consistent offering, your company must have consistent roles (collections of tasks). People will grow and people may go, but the roles will stay. Great leaders define the tasks for each role first, and then find the best person to fill that role.
Place Equal Importance on Each Quality and Qualification No human being will have every single attribute you need. Good leaders want the person who has the most qualities and qualifications for a role.	**Prioritize Specific Qualities and Qualifications** A person's potential is maximized when they lean in to a few talents. It's not about being well-rounded. Great leaders identify the few qualities and qualifications that will have the greatest impact in a role and find someone with those attributes.
Prioritize Experience Experience is relevant. It can be an indicator of ability and skill. Good leaders hire people who have enough experience to "hit the ground running" on day one.	**Prioritize Intangibles** You can give someone experience, but you will never be able to change the intangibles. Great leaders prioritize hiring for intangibles over experience.
Replace High Performers with Other High Performers When a high performer leaves the company, good leaders look for their replacement.	**Deconstruct High Performers into Distinct Tasks** Most employees do multiple tasks. High performers tend to do more tasks than others. When that person leaves, great leaders look at the tasks they were doing and separate them into categories. This is the process of "fractionalizing" a person's work. Then they transfer the individual elements of work to other team roles and multiple individuals.

3

Recruit Potential

'm not the mingling type. At conferences, I like to learn and leave. I listen to the presentations, take copious notes, and then find an empty corner table to scarf down lunch before anyone else arrives. I then head straight to my room to digest what I ate—and learned.

Luckily, my eat-up-and-get-out technique didn't go as planned this time. I was at a conference and the keynote speaker before lunch was Kip Tindell. He cofounded The Container Store in 1978 and was its heralded leader for decades, including when I met him. By 2004, when I saw him speak, they had thirty-three stores. Fifteen years later, there were about one hundred locations and more than five thousand employees. The business was lauded for its success with a banal offering. I mean, they sold containers, a pretty unremarkable product. Storage boxes are everywhere, and easily purchased at any big-box store.

Kip keynoted that day because he had found a way to help business leaders handle an issue that we all struggled with. The Container Store employees were exceptional—every single one of them. They were top shelf, A-players, rock stars, whatever you want to call them. They cared more. They worked harder. They acted like owners.

In his speech, Kip gave us strategies on how his company recruited his awesome team and nurtured them into even better employees. Everything he said made sense, but there was one thing that didn't compute. The Container Store paid higher wages than other retailers they competed with, like Walmart and Kmart. How could his relatively small business do it?

After the keynote, I did my usual thing and raced through the buffet. I found an empty table close to the door so I could eat and run. That's when someone sat next to me. It was Kip. Apparently, he also likes to quickly retire to his hotel room after grabbing a bite. I told Kip how much I valued his presentation, and he asked me what I liked most about it.

"I love how you have such talented people and can run circles around the Walmarts of the world, because your people care so much. But I'm confused. How do you afford paying them more? Aren't you buried in payroll costs?"

He chuckled. "I pay them more as individuals. But our payroll is less."

What the what? I put my fork down. "I don't get it. How can that be?"

That is when Kip took out a pen, grabbed the obligatory paper napkin, and drew this formula:

$$1A = 3B$$

$$1B = 3C$$

"There are rock-star employees," he explained. "We will call them the As. They prioritize the company. They see their work as a reflection of their character. To these folks, their job is their identity. They care about the company as if it is part of them. They bring every ounce of themselves to the table. To them their job is an opportunity to be their best selves.

"Then there are B-players. They prioritize their income. The job is a source of money which gives them the freedom to do what they really want. The Bs do what is necessary to earn their living and do what is required for the job. But they don't have an affinity toward the company. They may feel part of the company, but not that the company is part of them. They start on-time-ish, and they leave, both physically and emotionally, at the end of their shift.

"And lastly there are C-players. They prioritize everything over their work. To them, work is an obligation and nothing else. At best, these people do the minimum to remain employed and at worst are cancerous to an organization. They could care less about the company. They are ineffective at their work and cause disruption and distraction to fellow employees, vendors, and clients. This is the person you wish you never hired. To them their job is a necessary evil. And by default, your company is a necessary evil too."

Every business owner knows this breakdown well, even if we don't rank employees as As, Bs, or Cs. But what was Kip's secret to keeping the payroll down? A pay scale trick? An extra-long trial period? Skirting the law?

Pointing at the formula on the napkin, Kip continued. "As a general rule, I have found that one A-employee can get as much work accomplished as three B-employees. And one B-employee can do three times the work of a C-employee. The math works that one A-employee is as good as three Bs or nine Cs.

"Now, here's my 'secret.' I pay my A-employees one and half times the industry average, and I pack in great benefits and work environment. This is how I attract the best people to come and stay with The Container Store."

I was fascinated by what Kip was saying, but to me, it still sounded like overwhelming overhead. He paid his team even *more* than I expected *and* threw in tons of bennies. "This sounds amazing," I said, "but I still can't see it being economically feasible."

"It isn't feasible . . . for my competitors. You see, on the aggregate I pay less. Here's how it works. Walmart, for example, hires mostly B- and C-performers. Those people get paid, let's say, twenty dollars per hour for their work. I hire A-listers and pay them thirty-five dollars an hour. But the Walmarts of the world need minimally three people to deliver the same output as my one A-rated employee. They pay three people at twenty dollars an hour to get the same work done that one of my folks does. It costs Walmart at least sixty dollars an hour compared to my thirty-five per hour. I have better workers who love my customers and company, and my payroll costs are half of the big-box shops."

Here's Kip's formula again:

1 A-player: $35/hour

3 B-players: $60/hour ($20/hour × 3 employees = $60/hour)

9 C-players: $180/hour ($20/hour × 9 employees = $180/hour)

Ah, OK. Kip's strategy finally clicked for me. The cost of payroll is not for the volume of people but for the volume of *production*.

What matters is what the company can produce. It is like having a printer that can print one page per minute or seventy-five pages per minute. The second printer has far superior output, so it is clearly more valuable for people with a need for speed, and that's why those folks are willing to pay more for it.

But ordinary bosses don't see how this principle links to the staffing. Many will instead buy seventy-five printers, printing at one page a minute, to get the seventy-five-pages-per-minute output. It sounds absurd. All these printers take up tons of space and power. They all require maintenance and repair. So why would anyone do that? Because cheap printers are cheap, and they're everywhere, and let's be real, it's also because they're "disposable." That last reason may sound harsh, but I strongly suspect you know of leaders who see their team that way.

You can find a cheap printer anywhere, at any time. When the need strikes, there it is. Ironically, the seventy-five-pages-per-minute printers are also readily available. They simply aren't everywhere. You'll find them at a specialty outlet. You will need to do some research. You may need to make sure you have the right power source and space. You may need to do a little more work configuring them for your network. But once they are installed, the higher-output printers use less space, fewer resources, and less effort. You maintain one printer, not seventy-five, and the output is the same.

Recruit and develop the top-performing, high-potential folks and you will need fewer of them. Plus, they are the employees who see your company as an opportunity for them to be their best selves. They are the people who will care for your customers, their fellow employees, and your company at the highest level, because they are innately wired to perform at their highest level.

It turns out that in the aggregate, the best performers are also the least expensive. That is music to my frugal ears. An all-in team must also be a *profitable* team.

Hiring the best performers to fit the roles you clarified in chapter 2 is another matter. How do you find these rare individuals, these unicorns?

You begin by realizing they are not unicorns after all.

COULD EVERYONE BE AN A-PLAYER?

"A, B, or C—give me an A or they're not for me." So the little recruiting rhyme goes. Historical recruiting approaches categorize candidates and employees as A-, B-, or C-players. An A-player is defined as someone in the top 10 percent of talent available, at a given salary range. The strategy has since become ubiquitous, and few leaders use the categorization as originally intended. Most have boiled it down to an ineffective and, I think, damaging conclusion that people either have it or don't—and that almost no one has it. Which is exactly contrary to what Kip was telling me, even though he used those same popular labels.

We both had scarfed down our lunch, and before a single additional person sat at our table, Kip gave me one final secret. "You know what is funny about A-players?" He paused without expecting me to answer and then said, "Everyone is."

He continued, "Our competition believes A-players are the individuals who walk in with the preordained expertise and ability. They think A-players are 'plug and play.' But that is not the case. A-players are developed. Yes, they have raw potential, but it is the leader who matters most. Our store managers sniff out the potential in candidates and then set up the opportunity for them to express it in their role at The Container Store. Our team consists of aspiring actors, hospitality professionals, and retirees. We pave a path for them to practice acting skills on the job, playing kind characters. We empower the hospitality folks to experience a variety of atypical tasks, like managing new teams, while they themselves are new to the job. We give retirees the opportunity to socialize more. All to the benefit of expressing themselves fully, while delivering the highest-quality experience to our customers."

I thought, *My gosh, he's right.* The old-school mindset is that A-players are the minority, because the expectation is they need to show up 100 percent ready to go. But the reality is that most of the world are A-players in waiting, and a great leader's job is to develop them.

Kip expanded my vision that day. The world is packed with A-player potential. Yet most leaders are treating individuals as binary. You are either one of the 10 percent of applicants who have what it takes, or, more likely, one of the 90 percent who don't. The candidate is either a rarefied A-player or not.

I tested this notion with a community of forty business leaders during a training I gave on *All In*. The results were even worse than the publicly accepted standard. First, I asked the group if they considered themselves to be A-players. Ninety-five percent responded "Yes" or "Absolutely," and a few gave themselves "A+++" ratings. I then asked them to estimate what percentage of the population are A-players, and the exact same group responded with "5 percent." It was a sneaky second question that revealed a massive discrepancy— and a common misconception. How can everyone see themselves as A-players, yet say that practically no one else is an A-player?

The reality is they are all A-players. So are you. So are the people who work for you. Everyone is an A-player—when they are in roles where they can demonstrate their full potential, and when they have the right conditions to develop and reach that potential.

The people I surveyed are all A-players, and it is because they were all doing work that they selected and optimized for themselves. They were doing work that was a fit to their ability and they had safety and ownership in the work they did. They fit snuggly into the FASO Model. And when that happens, A-player-ship is revealed.

When you believe that a person is either an A-player or not, and that A-players are as rare as royalty in a mystical kingdom, your hiring approach amounts to kissing countless frogs until you find the prince. Hire slow, fire quickly. Keep searching and searching for the prince, and only then hire them. If you later see warts, your prince is actually a frog, and fire them as fast as you can.

In my not-so-humble and kinda in-your-face opinion, this way of thinking is rude, crude, and outdated. In the medieval days, bloodletting with leeches to fight disease was revered. Not effective but revered. Modern medicine has a far greater, albeit imperfect track record. Yet for more than three thousand years, leeches were the standard operating procedure for treating many ailments. Yeah, leeches have their place in the ecosystem, and in some very specific medical applications, but they are not and should not be the standard. So here is my ballsy statement: A, B, or C rankings of people may still be convenient vernacular, but it is a damned medieval standard for team building.

The "A-player/B-player" binary approach, where either you've got it or you don't, limits opportunities for building teams with new talent and strengthening teams with existing talent. This is because it relies heavily on assessing a person's intangible assets (e.g., their cultural fit) and experiential abilities (e.g., their résumé bullets), what they already have or proven they can do. It looks at the Oreo cookie wafers on the outside but ignores the cream in the middle, the good stuff. It doesn't consider potential abilities, how a human can be developed to be the best version of their true self. And it surely doesn't consider the most critical component of great leadership that inspires extraordinary performance.

I once shared a taxi with Jack Daly, a leading authority on sales organizations and strategies. As we crossed Quebec City on the way to the airport, I expressed my thoughts about A-B-C rankings.

Jack scoffed. "B-player salespeople will beat the pants off A-player salespeople if simply given the right processes in the right environment." He affirmed that A-player, B-player, and so forth is antiquated, and that leadership—setting up the right conditions to help employees realize their potential—is key to developing a top-performing team.

Jack added, "The only A-B-C rankings should be for leaders. An A-leader could transform an underperforming team, no matter how they would rank, into an all-star team. Similarly, a C-leader will destroy a team that is packed with top performers."

Ever read the book *Turn the Ship Around!?* In it, author L. David Marquet tells the story of how the Navy's worst-performing ship, full of C-players, became the best. Not a single person was replaced. Well, that's not 100 percent true. The captain was swapped with an A-leader. Shortly after, "Cs" turned into "As."

A modern approach to finding your best performers is to put potential ability on equal footing with talent assessments. Every human being has unexplored potential. Every single one of us. The question is, Does a person have an alignment of potential ability, existing strengths, and immediately needed skills that match the needs you have for the job and expectations? And can your business further amplify those strengths and give your employee new skills so that they perform at the highest level? Are you willing and able to afford the time to develop that person's potential? Are *you* the leader who commits to helping each employee become their greatest self?

EXPERIENTIAL, INNATE, AND POTENTIAL ABILITY

Assessing whether a person has what it takes to work for your company is about far more than their résumé and references. Résumés and references point to a candidate's experience, but give few insights into potential, character, values, and a list of intangible qualities. You want to hire people for the stuff that is baked into them, the stuff that can't be trained. The only thing you can give employees are the bullet points on their résumé: their experience. Instead, seek out top talent based on the intangibles and the "non-give-ables": innate and potential abilities.

Experiential abilities are the skills and experiences they have built up and list on their résumé. Innate abilities cannot be taught or "trained up." This is the stuff that comes naturally to them, and the way they are wired in terms of energy and attitude. Experiential abilities can grow. Innate abilities are fixed.

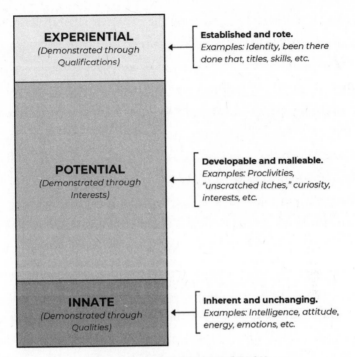

Figure 3.0 ▪ **THE TALENT STACK**

When we hire new employees, we primarily focus on their experiential abilities—the knowledge, skills, and experience they have acquired. We also focus on their innate abilities—the qualities they are born with and that have been nurtured by their environment. But assembling an all-in team requires you to focus on a third ability we often overlook—a person's potential, the strengths they *could* acquire in the right environment (that's on you), with the right conditions (also you), and under the right leadership (still you). Potential abilities are the things yet to be discovered by anyone, even the candidate themself.

Experiential abilities can accumulate when we explore potential abilities. Potential is malleable and can be developed and expanded. You can take a person's potential and fuel it with practice, training, and other experiences that develop the experiential abilities required for a specific role. On the flip side, it can be very hard to "untrain" experiential abilities that are not in service of your company or are in conflict in another way. So someone with less experience and more potential may be more valuable to your company, since they can quickly learn the skills they need in the way you need them.

Eddie Van Halen is one of the best rock guitar players of all time. He had innate talent, for sure. His father was a musician; he played the clarinet and piano. Eddie learned to play instruments without ever reading music, and even fooled his piano teacher's ears. That's innate.

Eddie, like all people, also had potential. He was born in Amsterdam, and his family emigrated to the United States when he was seven years old. He didn't know the language, so he and his brother, Alex, spent a lot of time by themselves, learning instruments. Music became their lingua franca, the way they communicated with and connected with the world. Potential is measured by availability, desire, and engagement in something. In one word, maximized potential is "thirst." The more someone thirsts to do something, the greater their talent can develop. The conditions Eddie and Alex experienced, though challenging, increased the brothers' musical potential.

Eddie's thirst for music helped him quickly gain a lot of experience. He moved from piano to drums, and when he realized Alex was a better percussionist, he switched his focus to guitar. This is when his innate and potential abilities went into experiential overdrive. Eddie started playing guitar up to fifteen hours a day. In comparison, I practice my guitar one hour a month—not even fifteen hours in a year. Is there any question who is going to be the better guitar player?

No one is born an expert. And the idea of having a gift is miscon-
strued. Expertise comes from repetition, and mastery from desire. So,
if I played guitar fifteen hours a day, for as many years as Eddie Van
Halen, would I be as good as him? No! Because, I don't have the
desire . . . aka the *thirst*.

The differences are the innate components. People who have the
innate potential and abilities have a natural "want" in them but not
necessarily the developed skills—yet. Desire makes the learning process more fun. Someone who wants to practice fifteen hours a day
will perform better than someone who is required or forced to do so.
Having a natural gift for something only translates to mastery when
there is insatiable desire.

Eddie and Alex formed the band Van Halen. They are credited
with bringing rock back to the forefront after the disco era, selling
seventy-five million albums worldwide, having thirteen number one
hits on the Billboard Mainstream Rock chart, and grossing more
than $324 million in concert sales. Eddie became a legend. Known
for his lightning-fast playing, he mastered a two-handed tapping
technique that gave us some of the most impressive guitar solos of all
time. When we limit our assessment of prospective and current employees to their experiential and innate abilities, it's easy to believe in
frogs and princes. We naturally buy into the belief that there are a
limited number of people on the planet who have the right mix to
serve our business at the highest level. While it is true that people are
not equal in ability, skill, energy, attitude, intelligence, and other intangibles, we need to consider more than just them. You need to consider your involvement in the development of their potential, because
that is exactly what great leaders do.

When you find a person with the right combination of experiential, innate, and potential ability, will you help them grow into the best performer for your team? Will you provide them with the environment, conditions, and support they need to reach their potential within your organization?

A successful fit is an employee who has or can develop the talents the company needs, is supported and encouraged by the boss, and is embraced by the company.

HOST WORKSHOPS

How do you find a customer service candidate with the potential to be your next greatest hire? Show them how to build a birdhouse.

On its face, Home Depot's free DIY workshops are a fun way to spend an afternoon and a terrific way to bring in customers. Learn how to build a birdhouse, rewire a lamp, lay tile in your bathroom. These workshops bring the community into their local store. But there is a brilliant secret agenda: it's a recruiting tool.

During the demonstration, a Home Depot team member observes the folks burning through the two-by-fours and wood glue to see if they'd be a good fit for a sales associate, or another floor position. Are they patient with themselves and others? Do they go out of their way to help other guests? Are they good at asking and answering questions? Are they super into woodworking, really geeking out about it?

In every workshop, you'll find people who want to learn something new, maybe make a Mother's Day gift (¡soy culpable!). These people are curious. And among them you'll find certain people who have more than a passing curiosity. Beyond basic skills level (experiential) and a pleasant, helpful demeanor (innate), workshops help Home Depot find people who have a genuine *interest* in DIY projects. That's where potential begins—with curiosity.

Potential always reveals itself in three stages. First there is curiosity, then desire, and ultimately thirst. Curiosity is the first indication of potential. Even if someone, in theory, has potential to be great at something, if they show no curiosity in learning more about it they aren't likely to explore it. Curiosity can either be satisfied or it can trigger growing interest, and that is desire. People with a desire to do something automatically seek to improve themselves and are more likely to quickly acquire the necessary skills to do that thing. At the highest level is thirst. This is where people "can't" stop themselves from learning and improving. These are the people who are most likely to become masters of the skill they learn.

In 2011, Domino's launched the Pizza Hero app, which challenged players to "make a pizza" on their iPads. The app was programmed to look for competency. The players who made the best pizzas were then offered a chance at a job at their local Domino's. Customers who had a general curiosity about making pizzas played the game, and those who had a genuine desire for making pizza *kept* playing the game; they perfected their virtual pizzas. As a result, Domino's recruited hundreds of new employees—people who weren't just looking for a job; they had the desire to make pizzas.

Always seek people who are curious, because they reveal potential. Narrow your candidates to those who show desire. Among them are the best talent for the job you have.

Hire for desire. This shows the application of potential. Desire can develop into a thirst. These people will become your elite performers.

Rather than post an ad, create an experience of your own. I call it a workshop. It could be a study group or a class. It could be an hour online, or a few days at your place. You could host it at the local college, as they provide necessary resources, or in conjunction with other companies where everyone pitches in. It could also be an open house, or an immersive tour of your facilities, or even a fun day with skill-growing games and social activities. Or it could be a simple, short, half-hour training and discussion. The event could be virtual or in-person, or a combination of both. The essence of a workshop is a hands-on, immersive experience in which people aren't just learning, they are doing.

At an entrepreneur gathering I facilitated in Tucson, Arizona, Russell Francis, the owner of CrossFit Jersey City (which he recently rebranded as JCFit) raised his hand. "Is this technique just for me, or may I tell the leadership at our CrossFit organization?"

"By all means share it and—" I started to say, but Russell was already out the door and out of earshot, on his way to call headquarters and share the workshop idea with leadership.

Truth be told, "mind-blowing" realizations don't usually translate into action. Sometimes people like the idea but aren't sure they can pull it off. Roadblock numero uno is that it's yet another task piled on a stack of existing tasks. How are you going to learn to organize a workshop? You don't have time to learn something new. And thank G, you don't need to.

Before I walk you through how to conduct a workshop, I'll give you a simple hack I learned from a stranger. After giving a keynote on *All In*, a guy approached me and said, "I figured out how anyone can do the workshop strategy—today. Be a participant. Go to a class and pay attention to the other students like you would if you were leading it." I didn't get his name. He just gave me that gold and left. Boom.

This genius hack reminded me of another example of finding extraordinary hires in only one day. Andrew Borg of Borg Design, Inc., a milling and manufacturing company in Boston, visited a trade school to talk with students. He then met with several of them and hired the three with the most potential. If you try this "guest speaker" twist on the workshop strategy, remember to build enough time for Q&A to identify the students with the deepest desire. Or choose to be a "secret shopper" student and attend the classes your candidates go to.

Technically, your company is already running workshop experiences. When you show clients how your product or service works, you're doing a demonstration. That is a mini workshop, and A-potentials will benefit from that demo too. Do you or your team members go out in the field and do the work? Hello, ride-alongs, the ultimate immersive one-on-one workshop used by firefighters and police officers. Do you have training that you offer your employees or take yourself? Boom! That's a workshop.

What about the cost? What about the time investment? Running immersive experiences sounds expensive. The reality is, you'll spend far less money and time running a workshop, open house, or training than you will following the traditional interviewing process. And even if you do end up spending more money and time, you are more likely to find employees who are all in for your company, which means they will perform well *and* stick around.

Before you overestimate the time and effort involved in workshops, and therefore abandon the idea, remember that the event is simply a learning and growth experience for individuals who want to explore their potential.

Also, workshops elevate everyone. Participants gain an education, explore their potential, and are empowered. Participants get to choose if they want to continue (an indication of desire) or have satisfied their curiosity. Some people will grow into what they discover—a big win. And others will see that this thing was not for them and continue down another path to find interest elsewhere—another big win. You are helping every candidate regardless of whether they end up being the right fit for your organization. The old "one person wins" interviewing approach only elevates one—the person hired. Everyone else is left to figure out "What's wrong with me?" and "Why didn't I measure up?" Not cool, man. Not cool. Let's do better.

When you're ready to try your own workshop, here are a few points to remember:

- A workshop can be any form of experiential training where people learn or enhance a skill.

- Participants are told it is an educational event (which it is), not a recruiting event (which it can turn out to be). They aren't candidates; they are students.

- When you tell people they are attending a recruiting event, they might try to impress you rather than follow their curiosity. When they start showing interest, desire, and thirst, this is when they reveal they are candidates.

- It could be a half hour, an hour, several hours, one day, or several days.

- It can be virtual or in-person.

- You can charge for it, or it can be free. Charging a fee, even just a small one, is a great tool to separate the tire kickers from the serious seekers.

- You don't need a large group. You can run one with just one person.

- As the participants learn through the workshop, observe people's curiosity, desire, or thirst—these are indicators of potential.

- Give students a certificate of accomplishment. Everyone is elevated and has proof.

- The goal of your first workshop is to make it as easy on you as possible. You can improve the next one, and the next, and so on. You don't need to have the skill to run it. If you do have the skill that you want candidates to learn, then teach it. Alternatively, hire an expert who does have the skill.

Now that you have the pointers, let's get busy setting up your own ultimate recruiting tool. Here's how to start your first workshop:

1. Identify the must-haves, the innate talents and established skills you need from your next all-in hire.

2. Identify the "must-develops." List the new skills that your all-in hire must gain while working with you.

3. Create an educational event that teaches the most important "must-develop" skill(s) and lists the "must-have" established skills as prerequisites. Design your training to give both instruction and experience.

4. Market the event. This is not something for the job boards. This is something you want to promote where people who are

curious about the skills you need already gather. People who have potential naturally gravitate toward their interests. Try associations, clubs, schools, and complementary educational events. You might also market your event to clients and vendors.

5. During the workshop, use the TIM method: teach, immerse, and monitor. Teach participants a new skill; immerse them in the experience of applying the skill; and monitor their ability, interest, and desire. Note who is most eager to learn.

6. For participants who would make good candidates for your open position, you may want to offer another, more advanced workshop at a later date.

SET UP A WORKSHOP		
Step 1	**Step 2**	**Step 3**
MUST-HAVE & DEVELOP	CREATE WORKSHOP	MARKET THE WORKSHOP
List must-have QUALIFICATIONS and must-have QUALITIES for students of the workshop. List the skills you can and must DEVELOP with candidates with the right potential.	Use must-have QUALIFICATIONS to create the workshop prerequisites. Use must-have QUALITIES to establish tests to reveal the qualities. Use the must DEVELOP skills to create a workshop that gives this instruction and experience.	Promote the workshop to the communities where the candidates with the must-have QUALIFICATIONS likely congregate. For example, associations, meetups, and the competition. In addition to the best training you can give, offer a certificate of completion and other accomplishment recognition.
Step 4	**Step 5**	**Step 6**
RUN THE WORKSHOP	APPROACH CANDIDATES	ADVANCED WORKSHOPS
Use the TIM method (teach, immerse, and monitor) to deliver the class. Make your best effort to serve each student while also observing the students to verify their QUALIFICATIONS and QUALITIES. Monitor for potential, displayed typically through curiosity, interest, and thirst.	Approach students who demonstrate the QUALIFICATIONS, QUALITIES, and DEVELOPABLE skills (potential) and explain that you noticed their abilities, and they would be a great candidate to work at your company.	Use advanced workshops to keep candidates engaged and to further rapport with candidates who cannot or should not be offered job opportunities at this time. Use Steps 1 through 5 to structure advanced workshops.

Figure 4.0

How to set up a workshop to recruit candidates with the qualifications, qualities, and potential your company seeks.

Throughout your workshop, identify the best candidates and move them into the assessment stage, which you will learn more about in the next chapter. These folks, of course, may not even know they are being quasi-evaluated. So simply explain to them, "We noticed how well you were doing at our event. We have some opportunities to work with our company in that capacity. Would you like to learn more about the company?"

I realize this new way of finding and recruiting candidates requires an up-front time investment that may seem too steep at the moment. You don't have to implement this strategy tomorrow, or even for your very next hire. Noodle it. Kick around a few ideas with your team. Start small. Big changes like this are doable when you break it all down and take your time.

Workshops are everywhere. The NFL finds top players this way. *American Idol* found Carrie Underwood, Adam Lambert, and Kelly Clarkson that way. And heck, the business world finds employees this way too. It's called internships. Shrink that internship down to a short format, and there you go. A workshop!*

GIVE THE SKILL TO FIND THE SKILL

Tuesday P. Brooks is a great leader who had a brilliant idea and matched it to flawless execution. The founder of AJOY Management Enterprise, a financial management advisory service in New York City, Tuesday believes the next generation of women in business deserves financial literacy, access, and freedom. She had long wanted to

---

* Getting workshops right is critical. If you'd like help designing your workshop, the ALL IN Company offers a Pathway Workshops program. Learn more at allincompany.com.

help educate young women in Africa so they could gain employment and start their own businesses. Inspiration meets opportunity.

When Tuesday learned that many US companies outsource accounting and bookkeeping services to India, she realized they could just as easily outsource to Africa. She also noticed that most of the established services in India served multiple clients, and though they were proficient in data entry, the folks she interviewed were not skilled in helping business owners navigate cash flow, improve profitability, and improve tax strategies. If she could train African professionals to provide the same specialized attention to business owners that her own company was known for, they would have an advantage in the global economy.

Tuesday partnered with a nonprofit and a professional Kenyan marathoner to recruit candidates for a bookkeeping certification—and The Phindiwe Business Academy was born. She started with eleven students and trained them virtually. All women, they were super engaged as they increased their skill set and ability. Those who passed her qualifying tests were given a certificate of accomplishment from Tuesday's firm, and she hired them to fill bookkeeping positions.

Not only is Tuesday fulfilling her mission to educate women, but she is also vetting them to find the cream of the crop for her own business. Her testing process allows her to assess their innate potential and experiential ability. As their teacher, she can see for herself if they have the innate ability to focus on details. She can also assess whether they have other potential abilities. And through her class, they are gaining experiential ability. By design, she is all in on her potential employees, right from the start. Everyone who participates in the program comes out with more abilities and consistently greater life opportunities. Tuesday's company wins with the perfect recruits. See? Everyone is elevated. Genius. Absolute genius.

Her story reminds me of a transformational conversation I once had with my good friend JB Blanchard. He decided to ride shotgun for a speech I was delivering at a college campus. As we walked through a building to get to the lecture hall, we passed several rooms with classes in session.

JB looked through the glass at one door, pointed, and said, "Oh, there's the best student," and kept walking before I could figure out who he meant.

About a minute or so later we looked in a different classroom and he said, "There's the greatest student." And kept walking.

A few more doors and he did it again. "Look. There's the best student."

I couldn't figure out his little stunt. Who was the best student that he could so quickly identify? Was it the kid sitting up front? Was it the person taking the most notes? Was it the student who raised their hand?

After he did this twice more, I said, "Okay. I give. Who is the best student?"

JB stopped at the door to the lecture hall and said, "Easy. The best student is always the teacher."

One surefire way to see if a candidate has the skill set you need is to ask them to teach you how to do it. This demonstrates that they have the type of ability you need.

RECRUIT FROM THE BENCH

The same Harris Interactive Poll that reports "bad hires" cost companies an average of $25,000 also noted that 38 percent of employers believe they hired wrongly because they were in a rush to fill the job. In my experience that number is well over 75 percent. We start looking for someone to fill a position when we have an imminent need, and that's part of the problem. When you run a job ad, you are hoping the stars will align so the exact people you need will be available *and* searching for a job. Why leave it up to fate? Also, let's face it: desperate leaders do desperate things. This is how we end up with so many bad hires (hello, Bahama-Fake-Dead-Grandma Elliott).

Rather than run an ad for an open position when you're behind the eight ball, start your process early. Keep a pool of names who could be candidates for positions when they become available. This is exactly how colleges recruit athletes. They run camps to teach athletes new skills and techniques. The colleges help improve the athletes and at the same time keep copious records on who could best fill their roster when they are in need. When the moment comes to recruit their next superstar, they use the list of athletes who have gone through the camps already and make their offer.

Sandwiched between the camps and offer day is a lot of communication. The college wants to stay top of mind with the best candidates, so when they make the offer, there is no need to rewarm the relationship. When I teach workshops about recruiting potential, this is where the biggest skeptics finally see the light. They recognize that colleges and professional teams have been using this approach for decades. The multibillion-dollar sports industry uses camps to compete for the most elite talent—and it works. If workshops are the secret to talent recruiting for world-class athletes, it will work for the pros in your industry too.

As an easy naming convention, we will call your recruiting pool in reserve "the bench." Another play on sports, the bench are the players who are ready to go at a moment's notice when another player leaves the field. You will have existing employees leave their roles or your company. And as your company grows, you will need more players in the field. Always have your bench ready.

To recruit from the bench, incorporate the workshops, open houses, camps, academies, classes, and other events like these into your quarterly schedule—even if you aren't looking to hire at that time. Your bench may also include people you meet at conferences or other events, or even your own customers. Remember, your bench will often have people who are employed elsewhere.

Danielle Mulvey, who I will more formally introduce you to in the next chapter, had one employee on her bench for eight years and another for two years. Just like a great college coach, Danielle would check in with them every few months to keep the connection alive. When she was ready to start her new company, she picked up the phone and scheduled quality and qualification assessments with them the same day. Both came on board, immediately. Both are top performers, consistently.

HOW CAN YOU TEACH WHAT YOU DON'T KNOW?

You might be thinking, "Hey Mr. Fancy Pants Mike, this workshop thing is cool and all, but how can I teach something I don't know? I need a marketer on our team because I suck at marketing. What do I do now?"

You make two good points: I do have a penchant for fancy pants, *and* if you don't have the skill, you can't teach it. But I have good news. You don't need to teach the skill; you can use an expert. Find a great marketer to teach your workshop. Shoot, maybe one of the candidates you are considering, someone who already has the abilities, can teach it. Now you can evaluate them teaching the workshop and the other candidates who attend to learn.

You will likely have to compensate the person who teaches, but trying to find people through the old method of going through résumés and "in or out" interviewing costs way more.

And if you want to be super slick, you can team with other leaders. Maybe you have a skill that other leaders seeking candidates need, and maybe they have skills that you want in your candidates. You do a workshop for them, and they do one for you. Talk about fancy pants—this is an entire walk-in closet of fanciness.

GOOD AND GREAT LEADERSHIP

Good Leaders	Great Leaders
Conduct Traditional Interviews Conducting interviews to find ideal candidates is a standard approach, and good leaders look for new ways to improve it. The challenge is, while you may find great people in this process, you may miss out on people who have the potential to perform even better in that role.	**Host Workshops** A workshop is an interactive educational event designed to find people who have genuine curiosity in the tasks you need performed. Great leaders know that many of the best candidates may not be actively looking or thinking about a new job. But if they have potential, they will always want to learn.
Prioritize Résumés and References Résumés state experiential and innate abilities. Good leaders also check references to confirm the abilities stated on résumés.	**Consider Potential Abilities** The most overlooked consideration in hiring is potential ability. Great leaders look beyond what a candidate has done in the past and ask, "What can the person do in the future?"
Recruit Early Spontaneous recruiting is highly susceptible to weak hires, which leads to a mismatch of fit and ability. Good leaders recruit early, before they have an immediate need.	**Recruit from the Bench** The bench is a community of candidates you have built over the years. It can be past employees, prior applicants, competitor employees, or people you have crossed paths with in life. Great leaders keep their bench full so they can streamline the recruiting process and fill roles faster.

4

Adopt the Five-Star Fit

I had a "genius" idea. To streamline my vetting process and give more people a chance, I decided to "interview" them all at once. I was inspired by *Survivor*, the reality show competition that made reality show competitions famous. If you've never seen it, a bunch of strangers agree to live in a remote location where they must fend for themselves to, well, survive. Kind of like castaways. Each episode, they are also put through a series of tests, and then one of them is voted off. At the end of the series, the "sole survivor" wins a million bucks.

My *Survivor*-style process involved having all candidates for a position come in at once, telling them about our company and our mission, and then running a battery of tests. For grand effect I had torches representing each candidate burning outside our entrance. To be clear, this was nothing like a workshop designed to find the candidates who had the most potential. This was a cutthroat reality TV–inspired competition, so I wore my toughest-looking outback costume, scuffed-up boots, khaki shirt, and all. I pitted the applicants against each other. If they won a comparative test, they "survived" another round. If they failed the test, their torch was extinguished and they were off my imaginary island. I thought my genius idea was so genius, even the applicants would think this was the best thing ever. Who doesn't want to be on fake *Survivor*?

No one does. That's who. The applicants did *not* appreciate it.

My concept wasn't all that bad, in that I was considering many people, not just one, but it was unfair to people who are introverts and people who didn't like public competition. They didn't perform well, or opted out, and I missed my chance to find out if they were the best person for the job. But that wasn't the worst part—oh, no.

As people failed the tests I gave them, I would "kick them off the island." This made it even more intense for the remaining candidates. And just as it happens on *Survivor*, that tension brought the worst in them. They formed quick alliances. They started to backstab each other. It got *ugly*. In the end, the "sole survivor" was me. I still hadn't filled the position; I was alone on an island of my own making.

And those torches I set up? I ran downstairs to extinguish the first one, Jeff Probst style, when the first candidate was kicked off the island, but they were all already out. Rain had passed through during round one and extinguished them all. Probably a divine indicator of the ridiculousness of my idea. And my attempt to relight the damp wicks was a demonstration of my bullheadedness.

Thankfully Danielle Mulvey taught me how to get *way* better at assessing potential candidates. No torches needed.

Danielle once had such a hard time hiring, she didn't want to come in to the office. The founder of The Maverick Group, an advertising and marketing agency in Nashville, Danielle discovered talent the way many business leaders do—on familiarity. She took recommendations and referrals from colleagues and friends and figured they'd "work out just like me."

Devon had a fresh design degree and seemed good on paper, but ultimately Danielle chose him for a graphic design position over another candidate because he was the brother of a good friend of hers from college. Almost immediately, he caused problems. Devon was combative within his own team. He believed work should be done his way or no way. He was completely wrong most of the time, and a total ass about it. So much so that Danielle did everything she could to avoid him. Despite this, she kept him on board, allowing him to show up for work while she hid out—anywhere but her office.

"I realized when it came to hiring, I was winging it," Danielle told me.

She vowed to make a change. Around the year 2000, Danielle started using the much more involved categorization system of evaluating candidates, and it helped tremendously. Over time, though, she realized she wanted to both expand the process to include assessments for an employee's potential and make the vetting process more efficient. Interviewing every single candidate thoroughly is time consuming. She needed a way to weed out people before she invested time in talking with them.

The Five-Star Fit was born. This method finds the individuals who have the innate abilities, potential abilities, and necessary experiential abilities that match the position you need to fill. Are they a good fit for the role's must-have list? Five-Star Fits have intangible qualities that complement the company.

How is the Five-Star Fit different than assigning letter grades to employees? Think of the rating system on travel booking sites. After your stay at a hotel, for example, you give it one to five stars. And your ratings are completely subjective—they are based on your needs and preferences. The same hotel, delivering the same experience, to two different people with their own unique preferences will result in very different ratings. The same place on the same day delivering the same experience can still earn both a five-star and a one-star rating.

On a trip to Florida, my wife, Krista, and I stayed at The Breakers in Palm Beach. We wanted a special once-in-a-lifetime getaway where we could relax and enjoy time together. The hotel is over-the-top swanky, so we didn't feel comfortable there. My wife said, "We were country mice in the big city." We gave it four stars because it fit our needs too much. Yes, too much.

While resting in our room, we had knocks on the door at least three times in just a few hours: once with the delivery of a special treat from the bakery, another when the manager stopped by to ensure everything was perfect, and another when room service offered to turn down our bed. The place is "great," but it wasn't my definition of relaxing. Plus, I didn't even know that "turning down" a bed was a real thing until I did some internet research.

On that same trip, we stayed one night at a Motel 6 in between destinations. We needed a clean, safe, no-frills place to sleep. We snoozed like logs. The hotel was quiet, no one knocked on the door, and they gave us two free bottles of water—all for $87. We gave the motel five stars because it delivered on our expectations on all counts.

I wouldn't be surprised if The Breakers received multiple five-star ratings from other guests the same day we gave it a four. My definition of "over-the-top swanky" is simply mine. For those who expected to be catered to at every turn, The Breakers nailed it for them. Similarly, Motel 6 might have forgotten to leave the light on for a guest, and that could be enough for a guest to slam them. The ratings are based on not just experience but the intersection of expectation and experience.

Just as a five-star hotel rating does not mean you will have a five-star experience, an A-player may not be an A-player for each role at your company. This is where the Five-Star Fit recruiting process comes in.

Typically, Five-Star Fits produce at least three times the investment in their payroll. They often require the least hand-holding (but do like to be engaged with and supported by management). Because her entire staff are Five-Star Fits, Danielle scaled her companies to more than $50 million in annual revenue while spending less than ten hours a week overseeing operations.

I like to tour offices. I have been to cookie factories, audiology operations, funeral homes, real estate firms, security stores, law practices, play set manufacturers, software shops—the list goes on and on. I always pay the most attention to the employees. What is their behavior like? How engaged are they? How connected are they to their team, their mission, their company? Of all the places I have been to, and it is well into the hundreds, Danielle's company had it all.

I'm not shy, so when I realized Danielle had the team of teams and was helping assemble them for other companies, I jumped on the obvious. I said, "I see what you have done here. I know people constantly ask you for your help building their teams. What if we partnered to create a business to serve anyone in need?"

Helloooooooo The ALL IN Company. If you want help in this process, you can get started by downloading your own copy of the Five-Star Fit overview at allinbymike.com.

THE FIVE-STAR FIT PROCESS

As we dig into this process, we need to agree to a principle. Everyone is an A-player. They simply need to be put in a role that allows them to express their full potential. Again, I am not saying that everyone is an A-player for *you*. And in the same breath, I am not saying only a select rare few are A-players for you. Everyone has potential. Everyone has A-potential. Your job, as a great leader, is to empower people to express their A-potential during the consideration process and determine if you have a fit for that potential in a way that it can be maximized.

Here's how the Five-Star Fit hiring process works:

Phase 1: The ALL IN Assessment. If you aren't ready to run workshops yet, this tool is another streamlined way to find the best candidates. In the job posting, applicants are informed that the vetting process is in five phases. The first step is to fill out the ALL IN Assessment, which takes roughly thirty-five minutes to complete. Essentially, you are saying, "Don't apply if you're not going to take the time to do this." According to Danielle, roughly 60 percent of applicants do not complete this step, and of those who do, 50 percent score low enough to drop out, which means you can devote your time to the top candidates. Similar to the effort of attending a workshop, the ALL IN Assessment requires a demonstration of true desire to follow through. This requirement is the second-most effective way to gauge desire, with workshops being the first.

During an ALL IN training, one of the students said, "That's such a pain for anyone applying. I know, for one, I wouldn't fill this out unless it was a job I really wanted." Exactly the point! We only want people who want it. Not the people who are doing blanket, click, and move-on responses to every job listing. When an applicant scores at least 70 percent on their ALL IN Assessment, they move on to Phase 2.

Phase 2: The screening interview. This is a baseline evaluation of no more than twenty minutes, done via phone or video. Most of the questions relate to the candidate's résumé, such as, "Why did you leave your last position?" "What do you like about your current position?" "What made you want to look for a new job?" Here, you are looking for interest and passion for the job they applied for. Although the max duration is twenty minutes, a screening interview could be as short as ninety seconds. No potential = no fit. Note: As you learned in the last chapter, running a workshop can be an efficient way to find the best candidates with the most potential. If you opt to run one, it replaces Phase 1 and Phase 2, so you can jump right to Phase 3.

Phase 3: The demonstration. In this phase, applicants take a skills test related to the responsibilities of their job. So if they are applying for a bookkeeping position, they would take a test to show their aptitude for debits and credits, another test for specific software, and a few tests where they have dialogue with and provide information to an individual posing as a client who has common problems real clients often have.

Phase 4: The Deep Dive Interview. By now, you have filtered out most of the one-, two-, and three-star matches. You have a good sense for a candidate's abilities. In this interview, ask about their future. What do they see for themselves, personally and professionally? What do they want? What are their dreams? Is there a future together? No one works for a company from the day they are born until the day they die. And even if they are long-term, they still have a life outside of work. So we walk the path of life together. Work life and life-life are commingled. Your job, should you hire this person, is to support to the best of your ability their life goals through the achievement of their work responsibilities.

After the interview, make sure to check references. Most interviewers neglect to call references, and that is a mistake. When they do call, the reference is afraid to say anything that could impede the candidate or introduce bias. So usually you just get the dates worked and maybe a title. I have a simple hack for this. Instead ask, "We have many different roles the person can serve in our organization. Assuming they can do anything they want to do here, what role (job/ tasks) do you feel this candidate would excel at most?" This one simple question opens the door for candid feedback on their A-player potential.

Phase 5: The shadow day. Candidates now have an opportunity to spend a day at your organization meeting the team and learning about the culture and how the job works. This is a paid offer. A shadow day may also involve additional skills tests in the form of small projects or assignments. If a candidate does well on their shadow day, you may then decide to offer them the position. It also exposes the candidate to your work community. They get a sense for what is expected from them and the vibe. And they can in almost all circumstances do the shadow day without having to quit employment elsewhere. They usually just take a day off. The candidate can decide if they want the position, just as you can decide to offer it.

You may be thinking, "Mike, I need to fill vacant positions ASAP. This process takes too long!"* My response is twofold: It takes roughly the same amount of time to start filling up your workshop event as it does to schedule your calendar for interviews. And the cost of bad hires is big. So slow your roll. And start looking for matches before you need to.

When you feel you are ready to get married, you don't start looking for someone to head to the altar with you tomorrow afternoon. Instead, you typically go through multiple experiences together to ensure you are both happy, then you get engaged, and then you later get married.

According to CareerBuilder, three out of four employers say they've hired the wrong person for a position, and 30 percent of them said this was because they felt pressured to fill the position quickly. Don't rush the execution of the process. But get the process started now, so you aren't rushed then.

The Five-Star Fit method weeds out all but the top 15 percent of best-matched applicants, so by using this approach, you are already ahead of the game. Kasey Anton, one of our all-in students, refers to the vetting process as "the gauntlet." It works. And it is light-years better than the typical "fog test" many panicked leaders use—as in, if you can fog a mirror with your breath, you get the job.

THE THREE KEY QUALITIES

Have you noticed that some travel booking websites have advanced rating systems beyond the overall five stars? They also have ratings for different categories—cleanliness, amenities, customer service,

---

* For help with the hiring process, visit allincompany.com to learn about services.

and so on. If I had spent a bit more time looking at those ratings, I might have figured out that Krista and I would feel like country mice at The Breakers and would be blown away by a middle-tier Hampton Inn. This is the overlap of expectation and experience.

In chapter 2, I asked you to come up with your must-have lists for your team. That list includes the qualities you need for each position. You may have different qualities for some of the positions because you have different expectations for those roles. And you likely have some of the same qualities for each position, qualities that match your company values.

I'll bet there is at least one must-have quality we all want in a hotel or motel: cleanliness. Read through the reviews for most hotels and you'll see that comments about cleanliness—good and bad—are the most common. There are some qualities that every role needs, no matter your company values. When I asked Danielle about this, she gave me the absolute must-haves for any role: limber, learn, and listen. If a candidate doesn't test well with these key three abilities, they are likely going to struggle to excel in your business, particularly in dynamic roles.

1. **Limber.** A candidate must demonstrate that they are ready and able to adapt to change. Can they adjust to changes? Are they ready and willing to be where they are needed? Will they serve the company in any way they can? A limber employee doesn't demonstrate their value through authority. They show their worth through contribution. For example, during the early months of the Covid-19 pandemic, MIT Endicott House, a conference center in Dedham, Massachusetts, had to shut down. Their entire hospitality staff of thirty maintained their salaries, because they were flexible about their jobs.

The cooking staff, maintenance, and housekeeping services all kept working. They became drivers who delivered takeout to MIT students who no longer had access to cafeterias. They became painters and renovators as they revamped the properties. They did whatever needed to be done when it needed to be done.

2. **Learn.** A candidate must demonstrate that they are willing to learn, that they are constantly looking to improve themselves through acquiring knowledge. They feel comfortable challenging their own beliefs. For example, my daughter, Adayla, studied biology in college. Now she is learning something completely different in her role at Penned with Purpose, a company that helps authors create, optimize, publish, and market their books using the methods that worked for me. Publishing is out of Adayla's wheelhouse, but because she's a learner, she has become quite the strategist. She closed her first deal with a major publisher within her first month on board. Yeah, Papa is proud.

3. **Listen.** Candidates must be good listeners. They must be able to take direction, but more than that, they must be able to listen *for* direction. Good listeners do not listen to reply or react. They listen to understand. They don't have an agenda; they are not in a rush to add thoughts. They summarize their understanding of what they've heard and conclude what was discussed. Good listeners follow up on the status of commitments. They seek to improve.

Effective listening is not passive, in one ear and out the other. It is learning, digesting, participating, and building on through response. Listening is key to any discussion, even in intense negotiations. As Chris Voss, author of *Never Split the Difference*, reveals in his book, empathy and understanding happen when you listen and understand more than just the other party's point of view, but their emotions too.

These three key qualities are innate abilities. They can't be taught. Candidates either have these abilities or they don't. You may have other non-negotiable intangibles for your candidates. It's important to think about what matters most to you and your organization, the abilities your business can't live without.

TEST FOR KEY QUALITIES

And old friend of mine, Becky Blanton, put me in touch with Jule Kucera, an adjunct instructor at the University of Cincinnati. Becky and Jule took a course together, and Becky, whose mind is a steel trap, suggested I talk with Jule about concepts I was testing for this book. In her former job at the University of Chicago Medical Center, Jule was responsible for designing the candidate selection process for a new department, and Becky recalled a mind-blowing recurring process Jule oversaw for the medical center back in the 1990s. It brought in the best group of candidates the organization ever recruited. And it was the most equitable process to boot.

I started off our conversation with the usual perfunctory question. You know, a warm-up. "What do you think about the job interview process most people use?"

Jule's response floored me. She said, "Job interviews are the perfect way to find someone whose job will be taking job interviews. Otherwise, interviews are useless."

My gosh. One question. One stinkin' question, to which I expected her to respond with something like, "They could be improved," or "Here's a great question to use." Nope. Not even close. Instead, Jule punched my question in the face, and threw in a little eye-poke as a bonus.

She went on to explain that when someone does well in an interview, all we really know is that they are great at interviewing, not that they would be great at any specific job (minus taking interviews). And she wasn't saying this hypothetically. She had the data. She went on to lead a real-world experience of running the same candidates through both the traditional interview process and testing just as I outlined above.

Jule told me about Chicago Medical Center's "Fit for Hire" program, which they launched in 1991. They needed twelve new clinic coordinator positions for the high-profile department. At the time, CMC was undergoing a downsizing. The union feared that the new positions would be disproportionately given to candidates who were white, given that the hiring manager was white. The hiring manager feared that the candidate pool would be filled with poor performers who were weeded out in the downsizing process. The union and the hiring manager asked Jule's department to come up with a better approach than traditional interviews.

For the Fit for Hire program, the hiring manager interviewed fifty-four applicants. She ranked the candidates and recorded her evaluations of which candidates to hire. But she held them in confidence until the next stage was complete.

Each candidate was then invited to participate at a series of stations that tested six key competencies such as accuracy, interaction with patients, and teamwork. Most stations could be completed in ten minutes, and the team-building station took thirty minutes. The testing took place over two days. Of the fifty-four candidates, all signed for up for the testing day.

At one station, applicants were tasked with checking "patients" in. The recruiting staff played the role of patients. For Jule's role, she chose to take on the characteristics of someone with cerebral palsy (CP), which she knew well, because her roommate had CP. She would take a full sixty seconds to get her clinic card out of her wallet. Some applicants waited patiently, others offered to help, and one person yanked the clinic card out of Jule's wallet in frustration. Two people angrily walked out, taking themselves out of consideration.

Upon completion of the testing day, the hiring manager revealed her interview rankings, which were then compared to the scenario rankings. Sure enough, the people who interviewed well didn't test well for the most part. The people who demonstrated the necessary patience and kindness needed for check-ins didn't do so well with (the job of) being interviewed. In fact, the number-one-ranked job interviewee was one of the people who walked out.

CMC hired based on the results of the skills test. And it just so happened that the twelve people they hired were all African American. It was the most equitable process the CMC had ever deployed; people were selected on demonstrable skills, and the best got the jobs. One year later, all twelve were still employed and categorically top performers in their roles, which had never happened before at CMC.

Who's the great leader here? Was it Jule? Maybe the union? I think the answer is yes to both. But there is one other person who showed the greatest leadership of all—the hiring manager. She had the courage to challenge her own assumptions and the confidence to believe she had a potential alternative to finding great people through interviews. She had the strength to participate in an activity that might just have proven her process wrong. And when it did, she embraced the new and better process. The hiring manager is the very definition of a great leader. And collectively, everyone showed great leadership.

TEST FOR FRUSTRATION

I've been the host for a couple of pilot shows that didn't get picked up. Shocking, I know. One was for the Discovery Channel, called *Go Big or Stay Home*. In the show, I worked with a couple who had lifelong dreams of being entrepreneurs. They wanted to own a bed-and-breakfast, but to do that, they would need to give up their current lives.

The husband, a car salesman, and the wife, a schoolteacher, had three children. They had a nice home, two cars, and a bit of savings. They represented a typical middle-class American family. I was about to give them the opportunity to turn it all in to live the entrepreneurial life. The episode started with me whisking them away for a few days to experience what it would be like to operate a bed-and-breakfast. This was an opportunity for them to really know what they were committing to.

That's when the hook of the show was revealed. While the couple was away, a liquidator came to their house and wrote a check to take immediate possession of everything they owned: their home, their cars, their clothes, even the food in the cabinets—everything. When the couple and I returned from the practice experience they were offered a choice: to go all in on their dream business by accepting the check and saying goodbye to their past life, or to rip up the check and return to life as they knew it.

To give the couple a real feel for running a B&B *and* to make the show as TV-showy as possible, the production crew intentionally presented problems to the couple. They switched keys, so that when it came to cleaning the rooms, they couldn't get into them. They clogged a toilet, which the couple had no idea how to fix. The couple seemed to handle those problems well. Where they lost it was breakfast. They had to cook for five couples visiting the bed-and-breakfast, and the stove burners stayed stuck on high. They burned the eggs. And the pancakes. True story: in a panic they finished off an omelet with powdered sugar. No, that problem was not staged. And, yes, that scene absolutely made it into the final cut.

After the experience, the couple decided not to go big, and instead stayed home. They gladly tore up a big old check when they saw how frustrating their dream work would be. Their curiosity was quenched, and the desire died. Frustration is the ultimate test of potential. It will arise for everyone, that is without question. The great leader observes how they respond. Does the frustration result in permanently giving up, or does it result in a break, reorganization, and trying again? And if necessary, trying again, again, and again. The latter indicates desire or even thirst; the former shows less or no potential.

You also need to run frustration tests with your candidates, since they reveal so much about their potential. Have people undergo an experience where there is a possibility of problems. Or compounding problems. The goal is to see how people respond. Do they give up? Do they get angry? Or do they rise to the occasion?

What is the leader's role? There is a popular video that circulated on the web called "Little Girl Determined to Jump the Box" or "Power of Not Giving Up," depending on where it is hosted. It shows a young girl, probably four years old or so, trying to do a standing leap to an elevated platform that is belly high. She tries again, and again, and again. Every time she fails, stumbles, and falls, she resets the platform and tries again. After nine failed tries she nails it. On her tenth attempt, she lands on top of the platform and screams in happiness at her success. Her father runs in and hugs and kisses her, cheering with her. An athlete in the making? Heck yes—potential revealed. Frustration managed. Dad's leadership? Pretty darn great. How can you tell? The joy they both express about her success. Great leaders support through frustration and celebrate overcoming obstacles.

The most revealing part of the video is something you won't see if you blink. When the dad comes in to celebrate his daughter's efforts, they go for a double high-five and miss. She almost falls off the platform, but he catches her. The celebration continues unabated with hugs, kisses, and cheering. This is the greatest part of leadership— there is not an expectation for perfection throughout. Great leaders allow the mistakes that don't really matter and celebrate the achieved outcome even, or especially, if the path there is fraught with micro- mistakes, failures, and setbacks. That is how great leaders cultivate potential and celebrate progress.

ASK ABOUT THEIR DREAMS

In Phase 4 of the Five-Star Fit method, the Deep Dive Interview, you will determine if a candidate's goals for their future line up with your company's goals. What does the candidate want for themselves and their lives? What are their big and/or little dreams?

Everyone has a dream. Some have grand dreams, some have small dreams, some have pipe dreams. But we all have a vision for our lives. The secret to an unstoppable team is to align the goals of the business as much as possible with the goals of the individuals. I am not saying to necessarily change the company goals around what everyone wants. What I am saying is to do your best to empower the achievement of individual goals and dreams, while collectively marching toward the company goals.

The goals of an organization are typically the goal of the primary leader or leaders. I know in my own business that when I set revenue goals and other objectives, it is first and foremost about my own desires. What those numbers mean to me. What those goals, when accomplished, provide me. That is all good. But to think that my team will have the same thirst to achieve those goals as me doesn't make sense. They are on their unique life's path, just as much as I am on mine, and you are on yours.

By knowing a candidate's personal goals and aspirations, in addition to their work goals, you can effectively plan a path toward their goals as you collectively move toward your corporate goals.

TRIAL PERIOD

During your assessment process, consider a short hire. Once a candidate has passed your tests, don't offer full-time employment. Offer a trial period instead, beyond the shadow day. It could be one week or up to ninety days. They will get paid and experience the daily operations of the company, and if at any time they realize it's not a fit for them, they can leave without notice. During this trial period you can get a realistic sense whether they are a good fit for your company. If they are not, you can end the employment after the end of the agreed upon trial period. Win-win.

MAKING THE OFFER

Payroll is the largest expense for most companies. It is generally a fixed cost. Whether you have a bad revenue month or a good revenue month, you still have to cover payroll. Before you make an offer to a candidate, you need to know compensation and expected return on payroll (ROP). You likely have heard of ROI (return on investment), but have you heard of ROP? If not, know this: ROP is a key metric to measure the health of your company and the strength of your team. This is what your company can afford and expects in return. ROP translates to the profitability and sustainability of the business. And it also reflects happiness. People can only produce at the highest levels on a sustained basis if the work is fueling them.

To calculate ROP, divide your total business revenue by the total wages. A fiscally healthy business has a minimum of three times return on wages. So if your company's annual salaries are $100,000, you should have at least $300,000 in revenue.

Compensation is not a motivator, but it surely is a demotivator. Meaning, yes, you can attract people with more money than the competition offers, but it won't make them work harder or smarter. They will do their best if they feel they are being treated fairly and you have an environment where they can explore and develop their potential. But if you pay less than they feel they are worth, they will be demotivated. You are taking advantage of them, in their eyes. Use what we learned from Kip of The Container Store. Pay 1.25 times to 1.5 times the industry average and it will be a rare occasion when someone leaves you due to a money decision.

To be competitive, you are best served to be "in the ballpark" on foundational expectations and needs—health benefits, vacation and other paid time off, training—but it is in the unique/extreme benefits where you will stand out. For example, flex time, personal time, the ability to take a sabbatical or work a four-day week.

Beyond time off, profit sharing, the ability to work from home, time to pursue creative interests, opportunities to grow in the job, and access to company resources sweeten the deal. Consider all you learned about your candidate in the Deep Dive Interview. How can you help them get more of what they want through their job? How can you further facilitate their personal dreams and intentions? (More on this later.)

Also, don't save the recognition and awards for a "surprise" once they are hired. Let them know you have a reward system in place when you make the offer. And have you considered the people they will work with as a benefit? Not just coworkers, but vendors, clients, mentors, and teachers who provide training?

Once you have an offer ready to present, don't oversell the role. The nice thing is, if you followed this process, it is nearly impossible to oversell. The scenario testing, skill testing, and shadow day experiences give them a full sense of the job and its requirements. A 2022 survey by The Muse found that of twenty-five hundred US employees who left their job for an offer from another company, 72 percent said "their new role or company was very different from what they had been led to believe, and more than half of them regretted leaving their former job." Someone who regrets coming on board is an employee who will never produce optimally, and surely won't have their heart in the game. But if they have already had hands-on experience from workshops all the way to shadow days, they will be prepared for any problems or frustrations, that present themselves. And their heart will be in it.

GOOD AND GREAT LEADERSHIP

Good Leaders	Great Leaders
Inquire About Skills Some candidates claim to have skills they may not have or may not do well. Good leaders ask them about their skills and confirm them with references.	**Conduct Skills Assessments** Even honest candidates may not have an accurate assessment of their skills, and references may not know the depth of skill required for the role you aim to fill. Great leaders confirm that candidates have the skills they need through demonstrations and testing.
Interview All Qualified Candidates First Once you've confirmed a candidate has the ability to fit into your role, interviewing all qualified candidates is the next logical step. Good leaders interview as many candidates as possible.	**Conduct ALL IN Assessments First** Not every candidate should be given equal time in consideration. Some apply for many jobs and don't have a genuine interest in working for your company. Great leaders conduct workshops, and when they opt not to do that, they require ALL IN Assessments as the first step in the hiring process.
Calculate Salary Affordability Traditional budgeting treats employees as an expense. Good leaders consider, "Can we afford to make the hire?"	**Calculate Return on Payroll (ROP)** Employees are an investment. Great leaders know there must be an expected return on their investment, since it is the only way the business can ensure it earns more than it spends.

5

Maintain a Secure and Accepting Environment

Some business initiatives work like a charm. Others invoke such panic in a man that, during a blizzard, he abandons his car in the middle of the road, engine still running, jumps a roadway divider, and sprints to the nearest building like someone out of a horror movie.

A former employee of Mars, Inc., maker of some of the most popular candies in the world—Snickers, M&M's, Skittles, and more—shared this story with me. I'll call her Charlie, after the kid in *Charlie and the Chocolate Factory* by Roald Dahl. That kid sure saw some crazy stuff he couldn't talk about. Mars, Inc. is a privately owned company, with two brothers at the helm at the time—Forrest and Frank. At one point, they launched an initiative to improve workday start times, the Punctuality Bonus. Everyone at the company punched in at the beginning of their day, including the managers and the brothers. With the new program, if you punched in before your start time, you'd get an additional 5 percent of your day's wages added to your paycheck.

Forrest and Frank had good intentions with the Punctuality Bonus, and it seemed like a good way to improve work results. But it quickly collapsed. Employees didn't see it as extra cash for showing up early; they saw *not* getting money when they *didn't* show up early as a punishment. People didn't feel rewarded. They felt ripped off.

This caused employees to arrange to punch in for each other, which then became a terminatable offense. Now, not only were you being punished for being late, but you could be fired if there was suspicion around you being early. And people who were already coming in early on their own accord saw no benefit in doing so anymore and so they showed up just before start time. Both the early birds and the perpetually tardy sought ways to game the system. The brothers responded by hiring a security guard to stare down people at the punch-in clock and make sure no one cheated.

All this monitoring resulted in the entire staff pouring in at 7:59 a.m., waiting in line to punch in. Arguments broke out among employees who were concerned they wouldn't get their bonus because the line was too long. Is it any wonder the staff called the program the "Punc Bonus" (pronounced "punk")?

And one dude jeopardized people's lives because of the initiative. Out of a desire to be fair to all employees, the on-time arrival standard was set for the brothers too. This is how Frank, or possibly Forrest—Charlie was fuzzy on which brother did this—ended up abandoning a car and racing through a snowstorm as though he was being chased by a serial killer. Frank didn't want his brother or staff to see him come in late, but traffic was slow due to the snowstorm, and he was at the mercy of the cars in front of him. In desperation, Frank abandoned his idling car in the road, jumped over the median, crossed in front of oncoming traffic, and ran through snowdrifts to stand in line to punch in. He risked his life, and the lives of other drivers, just to arrive before eight.

The Punctuality Bonus program was an abject failure, and Mars, Inc. eventually abandoned it. But that's not the end of the story. The cancellation of the program only upset people more. Because even though the enforcement system didn't work, and in fact caused harm, the staff still felt as though 5 percent of their income had been taken away. Ultimately, the initiative failed because it was unsafe for employees on three levels: physical (driving—or running—recklessly to work on time, arguments that could escalate to fights), psychological (multiple punishments, a distrustful guard, and even spies among them), and financial (losing a bonus that could make a difference in employees' lives). It was a triple whammy.

It's not uncommon for policies or initiatives designed for good reasons to garner negative results. Sociologist Robert K. Merton popularized the term "unintended consequences," which are "outcomes of a purposeful action that are not intended or foreseen." Unintended consequences can be positive, of course. The term for that is "unintended benefits." Bonus! The other two types are both negative. Like an "un-bonus."

"Unintended drawbacks" is when a positive outcome also has a negative component. An example of this would be the "three strikes law," which doles out harsher punishments to repeat offenders. In California, the law did reduce overall crime somewhat, but had one terrible unintended drawback: violent crimes increased. This was due in part to the fact that the law "flattened the penalty gradient with respect to severity."

Finally, there is "perverse result," which is when the solution to a problem actually makes it worse. In Australia, a study showed that a vegetarian diet may be responsible for twenty-five times as many animal deaths as a carnivorous diet. More tractors reaping crops crush rodents and other wild animals, thus posing the difficult question: Which life is more valuable, that of the mouse or that of the cow?

But was Frank and Forrest's good intent good enough? They certainly didn't set out to harm their employees—or themselves—with a bonus plan. And yet their initiative had an unintended drawback.

Great leaders look for unintended consequences when they create policies and monitor for them after implementation, especially those that may affect their employees' safety. As my mother says, "Everyone is smart. A few before and most after." Consider how your company's policies, programs, and general work environment will impact your employees' sense of physical, psychological, and financial safety. When your team feels unsafe in any one of these areas it can affect every aspect of their work experience and limit their potential. When they feel safe in all three areas, they are not only willing to be all in for your business; they *want* to be all in.

PHYSICAL SAFETY

"Ghost Girls" was the name people gave the women who worked in factories after World War I making watches and military dials using radium. When they left work at night after a long shift, their clothes and skin glowed in the dark. They used a precision painting technique that required them to dip a paintbrush in glowing green paint, then put the brush between their lips to make as fine a point as possible. They repeated this process throughout the day, each time swallowing a small amount of radium-laden paint. When one of the Ghost Girls asked if the paint would hurt them, their manager told them it wasn't dangerous and they "did not need to be afraid."

Of course, we know radium is radioactive, and it began to destroy the factory workers from the inside. That glowing effect was not just on the outside—one doctor described a woman's "glowing bones." Dozens of women died from the exposure, and hundreds had lifelong illnesses and disabilities. The factory leaders knew of the health risks yet lied about the danger. Later, they orchestrated a cover-up. Still, the women who led the fight to hold the factory responsible persevered, and eventually won their legal case. It was the first time an employer was made accountable for the health of their employees and led to the establishment of the Occupational Safety and Health Administration (OSHA).

It seems like a no-brainer not to lie to your employees about their personal safety. Sometimes, though, we miss things. Maybe there are unintended consequences, or maybe we haven't considered another person's experience or perspective. Our own ignorance can get in the way of our team's well-being. For example, some workers may feel perfectly safe parking a few blocks away from work, while others may not. And the employees who seem to be in a "safe" job, such as knowledge workers, also need consideration of safe work conditions.

One of the brainstorms you can do at your quarterly or annual retreats is around physical safety. Ask your team to come up with ideas to enhance the safety of the work environment. Brainstorm what could be unsafe and build lists.

Use the services of your insurance company and invite them in for a safety check. My longest-term friend is Chris Forte. We have known each other since we were babies. We were neighbors and grew up together. Chris's first job out of college was with United States Fidelity & Guaranty (USF&G) doing site audits at different clients. When we hung out during holiday breaks, he would recount stories of "short-cuts" workers took to get more done, faster.

For example, at one factory, a bonus for cutting thick metal sheets faster led one employee to circumvent a safety device. Instead of having to put the material in the machine and then be forced to remove his hands to push two large safety buttons to initiate cutting, the employee duct-taped one button in the closed position. Now he could load the sheets with one hand and hit the other button with the other hand. Compromised safety was the unintended consequence of a bonus for working faster. And no one brought it up.

Chris cited the problem, and it was "fixed"—until he had to return because there was an accident. A worker had lost his hand in the cutting machine. The reason? The employee had retaped one of the safety buttons in the closed position. The company lost a worker, prospective employees, and tons of money because of a lawsuit. A great leader prioritizes safety and when they see it is being circumvented gets to the root cause and fixes it, even (or especially) if it means not cutting corners.

PSYCHOLOGICAL SAFETY

"Did you play sports in high school?"

It was a casual question during a typical watercooler conversation with a colleague. Still, Rhodes Perry froze. He didn't know how to answer it without putting himself in danger.

At the White House in the Office of Management and Budget (OMB), Rhodes managed an $11 billion budget. He loved his job, and he was good at it. But he was emotionally exhausted and disconnected from his team, largely due to seemingly benign everyday conversations with his colleagues.

"I was excited to answer the question, because I was an athlete," Rhodes told me in an interview for this book. "But my mind was doing this kind of mental gymnastics. In my heart I wanted to say, 'I played women's fast-pitch softball for sixteen years, and I was really good,' but I knew if I said that it would cause radical confusion with my colleague. I thought maybe I could say, 'I played baseball,' but that would be a lie. So I just settled with, 'I ran high school cross-country,' another sport I played."

Rhodes was socialized as a girl and a woman before he transitioned. In 2006, when he worked in President George W. Bush's administration, there were no legal protections for transgender people in government, and much less visibility. He felt unsafe disclosing his gender identity, which meant he ended up not sharing much about himself at all.

"I had to censor so much of myself, people never really got to know the best parts of who I am," Rhodes explained. "I had to brutally extract some of these things to fit in."

Today, Rhodes helps leaders in governmental, nonprofit, and corporate sectors build psychological safety, trust, and belonging in their organizations. He is the author of *Belonging at Work: Everyday Actions You Can Take to Cultivate an Inclusive Organization*. His research identified that not feeling safe at work impacts individuals in three ways: they don't feel seen, connected, or supported.

When employees don't feel safe to be themselves in their job, it's impossible for them to be all in for your company. Beyond diversity and inclusion, your team may feel nervous to share their ideas, their concerns, and their conflicts for fear of retaliation, condemnation, ridicule, or being shut down. When they feel psychologically unsafe, the person you hired who had so much promise may never fully reach their potential.

Though it has been studied for decades, the term "psychological safety" was popularized by Amy Edmondson, Novartis Professor of

Leadership and Management at Harvard Business School and author of several books, including *The Fearless Organization: Creating Psychological Safety in the Workplace for Learning, Innovation, and Growth*. She defines it as "a belief that one will not be punished or humiliated for speaking up with ideas, questions, concerns, or mistakes, and that the team is safe for interpersonal risk-taking."

Google conducted a multiyear, multimillion-dollar study of more than a hundred teams, Project Aristotle, to get at the root of why some teams excel and others don't. They discovered that the key common denominator for high-performing teams is, you guessed it: psychological safety. This is increasingly important, as a recent *Harvard Business Review* study showed that "the time spent by managers and employees in collaborative activities has ballooned by 50 percent or more." We are spending more time communicating with each other at work, and if employees can't share openly without recrimination, it hampers the entire team.

Gena Cox is author of *Leading Inclusion: Drive Change Your Employees Can See and Feel*, which defines the leader's role in driving inclusion from the top of their organization. When I spoke with her for this book, she made a key distinction about diversity and inclusion initiatives that I have not forgotten: "What we're really talking about is leadership. You're either effectively leading an organization and everybody in it, or you're only leading a portion of them. And if you're only leading a portion of them, how would you ever consider yourself to be an effective leader?"

Rhodes's and Gena's work makes it clear that promoting psychological safety begins with the leader. When you take risks and demonstrate vulnerability, it lets your team know they can do the same. When you are willing to be wrong, to make mistakes, they can do the same. Show your team you want to learn more about them and their experience. Ask questions. Correct your behavior. Be humble and open to grow, evolve, and become more aware.

FINANCIAL SAFETY

In 2018, Gene Hammett, the founder of Core Elevation, Inc., started a study involving five thousand companies. These were small businesses that had stratospheric revenue growth over a relatively short period, typically three years. Fast growth can bring numerous challenges—financing the growth and finding talent to support that growth, to name just a couple. But the biggest challenge Hammett identified? Ensuring that their high-performing teams *continued* to be high-performing.

Some companies met these challenges and continued to grow, and yet many others remained stuck in the struggle. In his study, Hammett isolated the common denominators of high-performing teams that continued to perform well in hyper-fast-changing environments. He started with fifty-three companies in 2018, and as of this writing has surveyed more than five hundred.

The Core Elevation survey found six levers to high team engagement:

1. Mission Alignment—The company was doing something their employees care about, and as a result, their work matters to them.

2. Transparency—The company was honest with the team about the company's progress—the good news and the bad news.

As a result, the team celebrated the good and rallied around the bad.

3. Inclusion—The company involved the team with the creation of ideas, bringing about psychological ownership in those ideas.

4. Growth—The company challenged and pushed the team to learn and expand themselves, which empowered discovery and the development of potential.

5. Empowerment—The company empowered the team to make decisions and to feel safe to fail, enhancing psychological safety.

6. Mindset—The team had the right mindset to accept ownership of tasks, roles, solutions, and so on. You can't just give ownership to your team; they must accept it.

The findings may not be surprising, but the reveal of the biggest lever is mind-blowing—at least to me. It was item number two: transparency. Yep. More than 87 percent of companies surveyed indicated that transparency with employees had the biggest impact on retention and elevating team performance. Did you think, like me, that it would be mission alignment, or maybe empowerment? Nope. The number one performance influencer is the truth.

Sharing information about financials, and about successes and disappointments, helps build trust with employees. This supports research around open book management and the resulting employee engagement. I implement it in every company where I have ownership or influence. No, we don't share individual employee or owner

salaries, but we do share the collective costs, revenue, and profitability.

I have found that when I didn't share the numbers, my team
would assume them. When my prior company was doing $3 million
in revenue, the team assumed, "Mike is taking home three mil, and
I get a measly salary." In reality, I was spending $3.2 million to make
the $3 million. We were operating hand to mouth. With open books,
the team had a much better understanding of our fiscal health. And
I noticed the team started to care about the fiscal health of the company more, including my own financial welfare.

Sometimes we make assumptions about what our employees understand about our company's financial health. I know I did. Every
quarter we distribute 20 percent of the company's profits to employees, divided up equally. For me, this benefit contributed to psychological ownership. I assumed my team would feel more responsible
for the company's success, and that some would become more frugal
with expenses as a result. Kelsey and I also felt strongly that profit
distributions would be a way to honor employees for a job well done,
for their commitment to the company. Because we shared information about profit each quarter, I assumed we were an open book.

Then one quarter we had a significant drop in overall profitability. We also bought out an investor by distributing some of the profit
reserves. As a result, we announced to the team that they would have
a reduction in their profit distribution that quarter. Their response
surprised me. They were more concerned about me than they were
about their profit share. In fact, they weren't concerned about their
profit share at all.

For years, I had assumed the profit distribution was a great motivator, and that because we shared information about profit each

quarter, we were an open book with respect to finances. After we made the announcement, we learned that most employees didn't really know much, if anything, about the financial health of the company, though they did trust that all would be well.

Since this revelation, we implemented a "Monday Metrics" session. Every Monday we report our cash in and out and weekly financials, including month-to-dates and year-to-dates. Each employee shares their key numbers, and we show how it ties into the bigger financial picture. And at the beginning of the new year, we rolled out an updated dashboard that showed, among other things, the financial health of the business and made it visible to our staff.

SURVEY YOUR EMPLOYEES

Take a lesson from me—don't assume anything about your employees. I thought profit disbursements gave my team enough intimate knowledge to both foster a sense of ownership and financial safety, but I was off base. To ensure you know if you are providing physical, emotional, and psychological safety, survey your employees. Start with the list of questions below and modify as needed. Remember to foster psychological safety by protecting anonymity.

1. On a scale of 1 to 10, how physically safe do you feel at our company?

2. What could the company do to help you feel more physically safe at work?

3. On a scale of 1 to 10, how safe do you feel to be your authentic self at our company?

4. What could the company do to help you feel safe to be your authentic self at work?

5. On a scale of 1 to 10, how financially safe do you feel in your life?

6. What new things could the company do to help enhance your short- or long-term financial mastery?

GOOD AND GREAT LEADERSHIP

Good Leaders	Great Leaders
Provide Physical Safety Employees' physical safety is mandatory. Good leaders put in place policies and standards that ensure their team will be safe.	**Promote Physical Safety** Employees' physical safety is not static. Great leaders consider their employees' safety as times and technology evolve, and when making any new business decision.
Invest in DEI Programs Diversity, equity, and inclusion (DEI) programs are a step in the right direction. Good leaders know this is more than a box to be checked.	**Commit to Psychological Safety for All Employees** When people feel free to be themselves, they are more productive, collaborative, and more likely to stay at the company. Great leaders go beyond DEI to ensure employees can bring their whole selves to work.
Share Revenue Goals with Employees When a team understands revenue goals and the why behind them, they are more motivated to help you achieve them. Good leaders give their team targets and explain the impact those targets will have on the company.	**Use Transparency to Build Financial Safety for All Employees** Revenue goals are not enough. When people understand the finances of the business it reduces suspicions or misunderstanding. Great leaders reveal numbers without compromising their confidence and privacy and provide education to help their team understand the numbers.

6

Foster Psychological Ownership

Hold your applause." We hear it at every graduation. Until the last student receives their diploma, we are expected to keep our hands in our pockets and curb our desire to shout our graduate's name as if we are rooting for them at a pro wrestling match. It never works, but the enthusiastic cheering fades as the event drags on. Worst of all, some graduates get nothing but a one-hand air clap. In other words, silence.

At the Baltimore Museum of Art's reception for their new exhibition, "Guarding the Art," there was no dying enthusiasm. Quite the opposite. In the introduction I shared an anecdote about the exhibit curated by the museum's security guards. After investing months of work learning the process, choosing the art, and preparing the show for the public, they were finally ready to celebrate their accomplishment. In a room full of museum staff, board members, patrons, the guards, and their families and special friends, then Interim Codirector

Asma Naeem announced the guards' names and a few sentences about each of them. At each name she recited, the crowd went wild with cheers and applause. Not just the guard's loved ones—*the entire crowd*. For every single guard.

"They were so excited for themselves, and for each other, and for their families to be there," Amy Elias, BMA board trustee, told me. "I got chills. It was just beautiful."

This initiative, the brainchild of Elias, was not just a feel-good project to boost morale and attendance—which it did, on both counts. The "Guarding the Art" exhibit was designed to create an atmosphere of inclusion, acceptance, and diversity. "It was the right thing to do," Elias said. "It was the smart thing to do."

Anne Brown, senior director of communications at the museum, added, "We were looking at broadening the voices of authority in the museum, empowering the guards to have a more visible voice and have conversations with patrons about the art that they may not have had before."

And *that*, my friend, is why I wanted to interview Amy and Anne. They were looking to "broaden the voices of authority in the museum." The security guards spent more time with the art than did the curators, management, and the board combined. They spent hours studying the art, noticing how visitors interacted with it, and of course, doing their Primary Job: protecting the art. Shouldn't they have some authority over the art? Damn right they should.

When they were first approached with the idea, all the guards were excited, though some took a little longer to fully engage. "They got more and more into it as they realized they weren't just picking a piece of art," Elias said. "The project engaged them on all levels. They learned about art preservation, about the curation process, about hanging the art. They learned how the marketing works, how the museum creates education pieces about the art. They were part of the whole ecosystem."

After the exhibit, which ran from March through July 2022, Brown and Elias noticed a change in the guards. Brown said, "There was a greater feeling of ownership—not just of the objects, but of the entire museum."

The guards started interacting more with other museum staff, and the trustees. They came forward with ideas. And they took their Primary Job—protection—to the next level. Brown shared a story about Michael Jones, a guard who had worked at the BMA for eight years. For the "Guarding the Art" exhibit, Jones had chosen Émile-Antoine Bourdelle's bronze door knocker, *Head of Medusa*. Perhaps because it was once functional, visitors gave in to their impulse to touch and handle the piece. With his newfound "voice of authority," Jones felt empowered to take his Primary Job to the next level. He designed a case to protect the door knocker and positioned the piece so it would be in full view of the security camera.

"Everyone here has a custodial relationship with the art we live with day and night," he said in an article for *Next Avenue*. "I designed a special case and now the door knocker has a reverent presentation. Finally, she's safe."

Reverent presentation.

Finally, she's safe.

"She"?!

This is a team member who cares as much about the museum and its art as the founders did, as the director does, as the board of trustees and the donors do. Jones is all in for the BMA, in part because the museum's leaders took the critical last step in FASO—they fostered psychological ownership in their security staff. And Jones demonstrated the ultimate in personal significance: the humanization of an inanimate object. A hunk of metal became "she."

On its own, psychological ownership strategy can move employees to demonstrate remarkable investment in their job and the company's mission. When combined with the other elements of FASO—fit, ability, and safety—psychological ownership is such a powerful tool in building an unstoppable, all-in team, you may be shocked at the results it brings about.

PSYCHOLOGICAL OWNERSHIP 101

We owe much of the psychological ownership strategy concept to Jon Pierce—and a meatpacking plant. Professor emeritus of organization and management at the University of Minnesota Duluth, Pierce took time out of his busy snowshoeing and cross-country skiing schedule to chat with me about his research.

In the 1980s, Pierce's friend Scott Harrison told him he had purchased a meat processing plant with two partners with the intent to reopen it. They wanted to offer their new employees one-third of the of the firm's stock in an ESOP (employee stock ownership plan). Harrison had the legal and financial aspects covered, but they wanted to track the psychological impact as well. That's where Pierce came in.

"Not at all familiar with the employee ownership literature," Pierce said in an earlier interview for thescienceofownership.org, "I buried myself in the science of employee ownership; specifically, the work related to cooperative and ESOP arrangements . . . I came to realize that accompanying ownership, as a legal arrangement, was a set of 'ownership expectations.'"

Basically, when people have a sense of ownership, they expect to

1. have control over what is owned;

2. be informed about the status of what is owned; and

3. have the right to a portion of what is owned.

Pierce learned that, at the time, most ESOPs were focused solely on providing a "financial stake" in the organization and did not meet the other ownership expectations. In his book *Psychological Ownership and the Organizational Context*, Pierce points out that employee owners are *not* necessarily more motivated, satisfied, and productive than their counterparts at conventionally structured businesses who are not owners. Along with fellow UMD professors Stephen Rubenfeld and Susan Morgan, Pierce came to the realization that "ownership is also a psychological phenomenon as people come to a sense of ownership."

My own experience with ESOPs supports his theory. This strategy seems to get enhanced engagement initially, but unless employees have a sense of ownership beyond financial and legal, it flops. In fact, I have more often seen a sense of entitlement with ESOP employees than anything else. Their elevated performance or contribution does not endure, yet they feel they deserve more money and rewards from the company because they now own it legally. In this way, ESOPs can give you the opposite result than the one you intended. An unintentional negative consequence.

In 1991, Pierce, Rubenfeld, and Morgan published an article in the *Academy of Management Review*, "Employee Ownership: A

Conceptual Model of Process and Effects." In that article they referred to ownership as a "state of mind," and coined the term "psychological ownership." Pierce then devoted years of research to understanding and defining psychological ownership—what causes people to declare something as "mine" or "ours"—and then applied that research to organizations. He discovered that when employees feel a sense of ownership in their roles and the organization, their affinity toward the company defies logic. In other words, they are all in for the business, even if it doesn't make sense on paper.

When I asked Pierce how to foster psychological ownership, he said, "People are motivated differently, so psychological ownership is different for everyone." While this is true, there are three main ingredients you can use with your team:

1. **Control**: Allow employees to experience control over whatever it is you want them to feel ownership over. For example, you might make them the point person on a project, or the final signoff on purchases, or give them the power to set the schedule.

2. **Intimate Knowledge:** Provide them with "intimate knowledge"—the information only a person who "owns" their domain would know. For example, you might fill them in on a backstory others are not typically privy to, or allow them access to in-progress work, or train them on the intricacies of a process.

3. **Time and Effort:** Ensure they are invested into the "target," that which is owned. The more employees put themselves into something, the more they feel it is theirs. Time is the big one.

The longer you work on restoring that old motorcycle you bought online, the more you will feel ownership over it. But time is not the only investment; it can be financial investment, physical or mental effort, or giving it a piece of you. For example, Pierce compares this to personalizing your new home. Adding family photos, art, and other personal items makes you feel like the house you live in is your home.

To deploy psychological ownership with your team, focus on one of these three areas at first and work your way up to all three.

Pierce's research went deeper. In addition to individual psychological ownership, there is collective psychological ownership. This is where multiple people feel they collectively own a target ("this is ours"). He administered a series of surveys over time to measure how much control they felt. Collective psychological ownership resulted in a reduction of voluntary turnover and an increase in job satisfaction and job involvement. He told me, "Feelings of ownership of the job amplified like ripples to the team as a whole, and to the organization."

A year before our interview, Pierce retired after forty-four years at UMD. At the close of our call, I asked him if he missed the university. Pierce paused and then replied, "Well, I still go in a day or so a week. I just have so much invested in it. I can't give up my school or my office." Do you hear that? He can't give up *his* school or *his* office even though he technically never owned either.

WHY PSYCHOLOGICAL OWNERSHIP MATTERS

When we feel possessive of something ("this is mine"/"this is ours"), we generally have a better attitude toward it, and we treat it with more care than we would if we did not feel this way. I liken it to the difference between renting a car and owning a car.

From the moment you show your ID for the fourth time and wave goodbye to the rental agent who deactivates the rental parking demilitarized zone (you know, raising the gate, lowering the steel wall, and disabling the tire spikes as sirens blare), you treat that vehicle like a plaything. You floor it when the stoplight turns green and slam on the brakes when it turns red. You let it get dirty, so dirty. Heck, you probably look for a parking lot full of dirt so you can do donuts before you have to return the car. Just me on that last one? Fair. But you know you don't love up your rental the same way you would the car you own.

When you drive the car you own, you take care of it. You're likely gentler on the accelerator and the brakes. You make sure you're up to date with maintenance and you keep it clean. If you're like me, after a long trip you pat the dashboard and say, "Good job, baby."

Here's the interesting part: if you're like most people, you don't actually own your car. You have a bank loan. And until you make the last payment, that institution owns your car. So what you're experiencing when you feel possessive toward the car in your garage is not because you have legal ownership, it is because you have psychological ownership.

How does psychological ownership play a part in your business? Let's run down the (almost) immediate benefits:

Your Employees Will Protect and Defend

When we have a heightened sense of responsibility for, influence over, or time with something, we will go to greater lengths to protect and defend it. You already know about Michael Jones, the security guard at the Baltimore Museum of Art who built a box to protect the door knocker art piece. We can look to hardcore sports fans for another example. I have never met a Red Sox fan who isn't a jerk—says every Yankees fan. And vice versa. Sports are a great example of psychological ownership. The Red Sox fan has the personalized gear and dresses exactly how they want to show support for the team (control); they know player stats, stories, and little-known anecdotes (intimate knowledge); and they plan their lives around games (investment of time/effort)—all things that bring more and more psychological ownership.

When a team member has psychological ownership, they take measures to protect and defend their own. That is exactly what Cait Oakley did for her pet goose, Frankie. One day, a bald eagle swooped down and tried to take Frankie. Oakley lives in Saanich, British Columbia, in Canada. There are roughly seventy-five thousand geese in British Columbia and twenty thousand eagles, so people aren't generally risking themselves to save geese from eagle attacks. But because Oakley had psychological ownership of Frankie, she didn't hesitate to take on the eagle—even though she was breastfeeding her baby at the time. She took off after the eagle, cradling her baby in one arm while swooping her other arm to save Frankie. It was *her* goose and Frankie was part of *her* family, after all.

Or perhaps one of the most dramatic examples of psychological ownership we've seen in the early part of the twenty-first century—the Ukrainian people volunteering to fight to protect their country from the Russian invasion. This goes beyond love of country. Their psychological ownership is over an ideology—this is *our* land, not yours.

Psychological ownership also has its downsides. Fifteen years ago, I met the inventor of a product called Light Glove. It was a mouse for your hand, *The Matrix* style. And in 2005 it was ready for prime time, or so the creator believed. The inventor had spent a decade developing it (investment of time), had done hundreds of iterations (control), and he knew every single circuit of it (intimate knowledge). He had massive psychological ownership and would never give up on it. Too bad the world wasn't ready or desirous. The demand never presented itself, but the inventor kept pushing to sell his baby, all the way to bankruptcy. That's the power and the double-edged sword of psychological ownership. We can become territorial, which can lead to sunk cost syndrome, where we just keep going, not because there is any proof for demand, but because we already put so much into *our baby*.

Your Employees Will Take Better Care of Your Stuff— and Your Customers

For Steve Bousquet, it started with work gloves. The founder of American Landscape and Lawn Service in Connecticut, Steve wondered why his three sidewalk crews went through 120 work gloves every winter season. At a cost of $7 to $10 per pair, the expense to the company was roughly $1,000. Not a big number for a company that does millions in revenue each year. And yet the glove issue spoke to a bigger problem: many of his employees did not value the tools and equipment they used daily, and ultimately did not feel invested in the company's goals and mission.

So Steve took a simple step—he strengthened his sidewalk crew's psychological ownership of their work gloves. He didn't reprimand his employees. He didn't make a big announcement. He simply wrote their names on their gloves and put them back in their cubbies. Seemingly overnight, his crew stopped treating their gloves as disposable. The next season, they replaced only about a dozen gloves.

Instilling psychological ownership was as simple as adding a name to the gloves, so Steve tried this with a bigger issue: the wheelbarrows. For some time, his crew of five landscapers had routinely broken the handles on their wheelbarrows. When I asked him about this story, Steve said, "My shop guy kept asking, 'What are these guys doing to break all these handles?' And when I asked the crew, they just shrugged. Nobody knew."

Steve finally figured out they had been tossing the wheelbarrows off the mulch piles in their trucks, which damaged the handles. But he couldn't get any of them to fess up to it or stop doing it. When each wheelbarrow costs $250 to replace, that's a hefty price tag.

To solve the issue, Steve gave each crew two wheelbarrows and put all their names on each one. This time he announced the change and told them they were effectively the owners of their wheelbarrows. You can probably guess what happened—no more broken handles.

Then an interesting shift happened. Steve said, "The crew started asking for more ownership. It started with hammer bags. Each one held $700 to $1,500 worth of heavy-duty hammers, the kind you use to trim rocks to get a nice smooth edge."

In the past, the crew would borrow each other's hammers, forget to return them, and dispose of broken tools. Steve gave each of them their own hammer bag with their name on it, and to solve the borrowing issue, he color-coded the hammer handles to match the color of their truck. One guy had orange, another blue, another red, and so on. He also did this with their other lawn care tools.

Once again, Steve's employees' behavior toward the equipment changed dramatically. They took better care of their tools, which they could easily identify based on color. They started repairing their broken tools rather than throwing them away. For example, one guy had a pitchfork, valued at around $140. One of the tines had broken off, and so he had it welded back on. This seemed absurd to me. Why go to the trouble of welding a pitchfork? Steve explained, "It was his tool, and he wanted his baby back."

Ukrainians are fighting for *their* land. Oakley is saving *her* goose. And Steve's team member is repairing *his* gear.

With a crew of around thirty, Steve said the cost to replace the gloves, wheelbarrows, and other tools was not the only point. It was the frustration he felt dealing with the issue, and the friction points his crew experienced on the job. When his employees started taking better care of their tools and equipment, they also took better care of the clients' properties.

"Taking care of stuff becomes a mindset, and it starts with the little things," Steve said. "I visit a lot of companies, and when I show up and see trash by the front door, the first thing I think is, 'What else aren't they taking care of?' When my guys take care of their own tools, and their own trucks, they are also taking care of my customers. If there's garbage at one of the properties, even if it's not ours, my guys will pick it up. They'll pick up a pile of leaves, even if they are at the site for a different project."

As a result of these simple changes toward fostering psychological ownership, customer callbacks (complaints) are way down, and Steve's company has the highest production rate in lawn care applications in the country. They earn $350,000 in revenue for each crew member, compared to the industry average of $220,000. And their employee retention rate is 90 percent. In an industry that typically has high turnover, most of their crew has been with the company for more than a decade.

Psychological ownership often starts with *my* things and then naturally expands to *our* things. The numbers don't lie. Psychological ownership works both individually and collectively.

Your Employees Will Stay

John Briggs almost lost one of his best. Sapphire Miranda, tax manager for John's Utah-based firm, Incite Tax, is responsible for ensuring the accountants on her team are successful in their positions and in their future growth. She had one major issue with her job: one of the accountants she managed was not very nice and frequently brought complaints about her to John and other senior staff.

"It wasn't this person, per se, because I can deal with almost anybody," Sapphire told me. "What sent me over the edge was John and our marketing manager kept meeting with this accountant without me. In my opinion, they were undermining me and training this person to not have any respect for me."

Sapphire is a rock climber, and during this time she noticed an opening for a CFO position at her local climbing gym. She applied for the position, and after she completed her second interview, she let John know she planned to move on.

"John said, 'You're not leaving.' He really didn't have any choice in the matter, but that opened the door for us to have a conversation. I said, 'Either you trust me in this position, or you don't. Your actions have shown that you don't trust me. I'll go where people respect me.'"

In trying to be a good leader and solve all the problems, John had

unintentionally taken away two of the three components of psychological ownership: control and intimate knowledge. Sapphire had no
ability to solve the issue with the accountant herself, and she had
no idea what had transpired in the meetings.

John apologized for letting the situation "get to this point." He
explained that he was still learning how to manage a growing business, and they talked about how to move forward. Sapphire told
him, "If I'm going to run this department, I'm going to run all of it
and I'm going to expect you to support me."

John agreed, and ensured that going forward, Sapphire would (a)
have control over *her* department, (b) have intimate knowledge about
their firm, *their* people, and anything that pertained to *her* department, and (c) make *her* department the way she envisioned.

Since Sapphire has had full psychological ownership of her department, she's been knocking it out of the park. As John put it, her
work is "skyrocketing." So is the department.

Sapphire said, "Now that I have this freedom, I am constantly
strategizing for the firm. I was on the commute in today, and I will
be on the drive out."

Your Employees Will Solve Problems Without You

One of my favorite examples of psychological ownership is the famed
Jungle Cruise at Disneyland. The ride started in 1955, and it was
originally supposed to feature live animals. Instead, Disney used an-
imatronic animals that clearly did not look real and then proceeded
to give the most boring commentary, as if the animals were in fact
real. Sounds like twenty minutes you'd remember forever—and never
get back.

It was the boat drivers who solved the issue. They felt a sense of

ownership over their boats and the tours, and they started addressing the elephant in the room (pardon the pun). They made silly comments about "lifelike" animals. They started coming up with their
own puns and "dad" jokes. Soon the ride became a must-do at Disneyland, with long lines waiting to go on the wacky ride. It's one of
the longest-running Disney attractions, and it even spawned a movie.

When your employees feel a sense of ownership over their job,
they can and will solve problems for you. They can even solve most
of the problems so you can focus on leading your company.

When Steven King bought two meat market grocery stores in
the Texas Hill Country, he thought he was getting a "well-oiled machine." (I know the name Steven King in reference to meat markets
could send chills down your spine, but this is a different dude. The
guy whose stories scared the crap out of my entire generation spells
his name with a "ph.") Instead, he told me, "I was bombarded with
texts, calls, and questions about every single detail of the store. I
mean every stinking detail. Then it clicked. They didn't know me
and wanted to please me. I had to unload all the decisions from my
head to ownership on the staff's part."

Steven decided to treat each area of the store as its own real estate, and he would assign ownership of the area to different employees.
He started with Shyla Cottonware, an employee who had expressed
an interest in doing more. "We went to the soda fountain area, and I
explained the issues. We had order redundancy because when trucks
were unloaded, the beverage inventory was stuffed in nooks and
crannies all over the store. Also, customers found the flow of the
area to be confusing. I gave Shyla ownership of that area, and she
quickly reorganized, moved shelves, and had all the drink inventory
in one area near the fountain. From that day on, that area belonged
to Shyla."

Because he saw potential in Shyla—her curiosity backed by action—Steven taught her about margins, and about keeping inventory full, but lean. He explained that every foot of the store should produce money for the store. She took on the challenge and streamlined the ordering for the whole store. Soon, Steven promoted Shyla to front-of-house manager.

"The battle of any business is the bottleneck at the top," Steven said. "After I promoted Shyla, I started giving ownership of different areas of the store to different employees, one by one. Each person is tasked with running their area as efficiently as possible. I gave them an education on business principles, and then empowered them to make decisions about ordering and which catering customers we will take on. If product doesn't move, they prune it. If a catering customer doesn't fit our model to make money, they pass—and they handle it themselves."

Passing ownership to his employees allowed Steven to take a step back and see his business as a whole. He expanded the stores to serve prepared food and host live music, and the store became King's Texas Smokehouse. He now focuses on customer interactions and the bottom line. And he can count on his team to solve the big problems too.

"In 2022, when I was trying to solve supply chain issues, Shyla used her resources to locate needed items. Our kitchen manager worked with food vendors to find the best deals and keep production rolling. They had the ability to be creative and make adjustments—because they owned their areas."

Shyla has thrived in her role and inspired other employees to step up in their jobs. When I interviewed her to get her perspective, I asked her if she felt a sense of ownership of the store. Her response surprised me. "I don't think of it as my store because it's not mine, and that would be stealing. I think of it as my home."

I think of it as my home. That is the ultimate in psychological ownership.

"I want to be at the store for the foreseeable future," she added. "I want to do everything I can to make the store a great home for our guests to visit."

When I interviewed Shyla, it was her day off, and she was at her actual home. During our chat, the phone rang, and it was the smokehouse. I asked her if they called her often on her off days, and she said, "Yes, they do."

"That must be frustrating," I said.

"Not really," Shyla replied. "I love it, actually. I love that I am so important to the company. They don't really need me. They get it done right without me when I don't answer. When I can answer . . . it's just good to hear from my other home."

Your Employees Will Live Up to Their Potential—
Even the Tough Cases

Steven King's ownership strategy didn't just work with motivated employees like Shyla; it also worked with employees who were so challenging, he was at the end of his rope.

When he started at King's Texas Smokehouse, Joell Dudley didn't have much experience with any job. The first few months were rough. He didn't take pride in his work, he had no drive, and he didn't complete tasks. On more than one occasion, Steven had to send him home to change because his clothes were covered in grease; he'd been working on his car.

"I thought maybe the problem was me and I hadn't trained him well enough," Steven said. "Finally, I decided to give Joell one task and one area of responsibility, exclusively for him."

Steven took Joell to the beer cooler and showed him how he wanted it organized. He told him, "The *only* thing I'm going to check tomorrow is this beer cooler. If it's organized and shelved correctly, you can continue to work here."

The next day, the beer cooler was stocked and organized just as Steven had demonstrated, and Joell had even written the inventory of each beer case on the box. More important, he seemed to have a sense of pride about his work, for the very first time.

For the next week, Joell's only focus was the beer cooler, and he continued to do a good job. Then Steven said, "Hey, the sodas could be better, and since you did so well with the beer . . ." Joell reorganized the sodas and created a new system for storing them and stocking them. Every label faced front.

Steven found out that Joell was into theater. He had loved set design and lighting in high school. So Steven praised him for his good work and said, "Joell, this is your stage. Design this area to perform its best. The beer and soda coolers are officially yours."

Steven said Joell lit up and took on the task. "Officially yours" means he *owned* it!

From that moment forward, Joell sought out ways to take on more and more responsibility at the store. He is now the team leader of the kitchen crew. His workload has tripled—and he loves it. Joell manages quality control (food standards, fast turnaround, and so on) in the kitchen, ensures customers are having a good experience, keeps records, and manages the truck.

When I interviewed Joell for this story, he was eager to share that people travel from all over the world to visit the Smokehouse. He takes pride in his job, and his company. He also passes that pride on to the new employees when he trains them.

As we were hanging up, I asked Joell what he plans to do for the next stage in his life, and he told me he aspires to race cars—hence why he is always tinkering with his.

"King's will lose a great employee that day," I told him.

"No way," Joell replied without hesitation. "I will never leave them. I will always work for King's, somehow, some way. Even if I become a pro racer, I will still be working for *my* smokehouse."

PSYCHOLOGICAL OWNERSHIP STRATEGIES

From the stories in this chapter, you've already learned a few simple ways you can begin to foster psychological ownership in your employees:

- Give opportunities for your team to exercise their authority and opinion.

- Educate your team beyond the needs of their job.

- Rally your team around a shared ideal.

- Add employee names to tools, equipment, specific spaces.

- Adopt a hands-off approach to allow employees complete control of their job.

- Explain the impact of their work on the company's success.

- Use possessive phrases like "this is yours" and "you own this."

- Assign employees small areas of ownership to start and let them grow into it.

Here are a few more simple ways you can start using this strategy today:

- Make sure your employees understand why what they do matters. My team knows our mission is to "eradicate entrepreneurial poverty." We talk about the struggles entrepreneurs face, and how when they succeed, it serves us all. Entrepreneurial success is human success. As entrepreneurs go, so does the world. We truly believe, to our core, that we are serving humanity.

- Ask them to create a vision for their area of ownership. For example, in our office we assigned Erin ownership of our kitchenette. Then we asked her to show us "after" pictures. She cut pictures out of a magazine to demonstrate her vision for the new and improved kitchenette, rough-cut wood shelves and all.

- Allow your employees to give direction to an idea and set their own goals. Use questions as guardrails but let them lead the way. For example, rather than say, "You need to make ten sales calls a day," instead ask, "How many sales goals do you commit to making each day?" An even stronger approach is to tie the question to the employee's sense of self. To do this, ask, "How would you rate yourself as a salesperson? Are you in the top 50 percent, 30 percent, or 10 percent?" Then, building off their answer ask, "As an X-percent salesperson, how many sales goals do you commit to doing each day?" Because the employee assigns the idea and the ranking, they are more likely to own that perception *and* the commitment.

GOOD AND GREAT LEADERSHIP

Good Leaders	Great Leaders
Give Employees Responsibility When we micromanage our team, we hamper their productivity and potential. Good leaders give their employees responsibility and set expectations about how to execute it.	*Give Employees Psychological Ownership* When people have psychological ownership, they feel that the object (physical or immaterial, such as an idea or concept) is part of them. Therefore, they naturally care for it more. Great leaders give their team control over what to do and how to do it and hold them to their standard.

7

Establish a Retention Rhythm

He wasn't qualified for the job. He didn't have any experience in information technology (IT). And getting a green card was one of the main reasons he applied for the position in the first place. Still, he went on to become one of the most loyal, high-performing employees I've ever worked with.

Born and raised in India, Sankara Shanmugam was fresh out of college when he came to the United States looking for a new life. At our forensics company, the one that was eventually acquired by Robert Half International, we posted an ad looking for someone to fill the IT role. Like I said, Sankara had no IT experience. Still, there was something about him. In the interview, he listened intently, seemed eager to learn more about the company and the job, and expressed a willingness to do whatever it takes. You might remember the "three key qualities" from chapter 4: limber, learn, listen. Even without an explicit awareness of the importance of those things, I still recognized and valued these qualities in Sankara. He also had a genuine interest in IT.

Even though I knew Sankara wasn't experienced and might only stay with us long enough to get his green card, he oozed potential, so we hired him to work part-time. And talk about limber: Sankara was a real trooper. At the time, all the desks and cubicles were occupied by existing staff, and we didn't have typical office space for him. IT support is not much of a desk job; it's a lot of moving around the office. So for his immediate needs, we cleared a space and put a "desk" (a foldable picnic table) in the server room, until we could find him a permanent spot. And my gosh was that room hot. And loud. Like a balmy ninety degrees and hurricane noise hot and loud. The only way I could have made it more uncomfortable would have been to release a swarm of mosquitoes in the room. With more than twenty rack-mounted devices running at full speed, the tiny air vent had little effect. Ironically, the occasional mosquito found its way in from the outside via the vent. To his credit, dude did not complain.

Sankara learned all he could on the job. Every so often he worked with our forensic investigators, setting up their technology and configuring their software. The exposure to their work fueled Sankara's curiosity. Then he asked if he could help them with their work—during his free time, no less. My answer was, "Hell yes! But do it during your regular working hours." I always encouraged my team to explore other jobs within the company, to do things they were curious about—on my time and on my dime.

Sankara took off in his ability. He was so good at the forensic work that he quickly became one of our best analysts. And he parlayed a job that was supposed to be temporary into a career. Not only did he stay with us through challenging times of growth, but he also stayed on when our company was acquired by Robert Half International, and now he's one of the rock stars in the industry.

Chalk it up to reciprocity and a few other behavioral traits—when you seek out ways to serve your employees' future, they will seek ways to serve the company's future. Be genuinely interested in each teammate's growth and happiness and I bet your team will be genuinely interested in your growth and happiness.

One day, a group of us were working late at night cloning dozens of hard drives, a process that often includes a lot of observing and waiting. To pass the time that night, I threw out random "What would you do if . . ." questions. I asked Sankara what he'd do with the money if he ever won the lottery. I'll never forget his response. Without hesitation he said, "I'd put the money into our company." There was no "I'd live on a beach," no "Take this job and shove it." Nothing like that. Sankara would take the money and put it into the company . . . *so he could keep working.* Note that his words weren't "the company," they were "our company." He had collective psychological ownership. He believed in us so much, he wanted to do anything he could to help the business. Talk about being all in.

Going from a part-time "I need my green card" situation to "I want (not need) to do anything I can for this company" is the epitome of "retention." It was not by accident. It began with recognizing Sankara's potential and then creating an environment that encouraged him to explore that potential—from day one.

Those seemingly small or innocuous gestures of interest are the key. Like an earthquake under the ocean, the force is massive, but not easily visible on the surface. Pay attention to people's curiosity, regularly ask about their interests, and invite them to follow their desires. When it reveals itself, your job is to bring that power to the surface.

His first day on the job, I asked Sankara to shadow me. I personally introduced him to everyone on the team, and they showed him appreciation. When we finished the tour, I brought him to his fold-up desk in the server room. We had everything ready for him—his computer, his office supplies, a brand-new company coffee mug, and a stack of his own business cards. We had also framed one of the cards as a gift, and the entire team had signed the matting with a welcome note. I'll never forget the image of Sankara sitting at his desk behind the servers, staring at the framed gift. It was the first business card he'd ever had.

Now imagine if I had shown Sankara to his desk in that hot server room and said, "Here you go. Good luck!" What if no one had greeted him? What if nothing was ready for him? What if we hadn't made the effort to have his business cards ready *before* his first day of work? I'm sure he would have worked hard at the job, because that's innately the guy he is, but would he have followed his curiosity to become a top-performing part of the forensics team? Likely not. People move on from jobs where they fill in the gaps. They stay with jobs where the gaps in *their* life are fulfilled.

Over the years, I've developed what I call a "Retention Rhythm," a method for connecting with employees to ensure their job serves them so much, they would only leave if their potential calls them elsewhere. I had some components of this in place when Sankara worked for our company. Since then, I have discovered, developed, and deployed more components. Collectively they have yielded impressive results. The Retention Rhythm starts before a new employee's first day.

T-MINUS ONE MONTH

Like when a college sends you a folder full of stuff you need to know after you register, send a welcome kit to your new hire after they accept the position. Ideally, you want this kit to arrive one month before your new employee's first day of work, but if they will start sooner than one month, send it right away.

Include an official welcome letter with the following information:

- Work hours and objectives (what is expected)

- Office and virtual protocols (attire and attendance)

- Start date, time, and location (physical address and links)

- Terms (ninety-day trial, two-year commitment, "at will" employment, etc.)

- Compensation (including bonuses and annual raises)

- Other benefits (health insurance, retirement, etc.)

- Contacts (emails and phone numbers of people they report to)

Include paperwork they will need to review and sign, such as:

- W-2 and I-9 forms

- Health insurance forms

- Company policies

- Equipment forms that specify the technology that will be assigned to the employee as part of their job (computer, laptop, iPad, etc.) and that at the conclusion of employment will need to be returned within twenty-four hours

- Acknowledgment that the company's intellectual property (client database, operating procedures and technology, inventions, frameworks and processes, written content, etc.) belongs to the company

T-MINUS ONE WEEK

One week from a new employee's start date, ask their manager to give them a call. Reiterate how excited the team is for them to join. Give the employee any final details about their first day, such as when and where to meet. For remote workers, send a confirmation with video conference links. Send all links for email, calendar, and system log-ons, noting that they will be activated on the first day of employment. And finally, if you require your team to wear uniforms, send any necessary gear.

DAY ONE

"How was your first day?" This is the number one question a new employee will hear from someone in their world—their significant other, a friend, a parent, their child—after their first day of work.

You have just one shot to make a first impression, and that impression lasts a long time. For Sankara, his first day helped shape his viewpoint of our company—he was all in from that point forward. I'm not just saying that. Twenty years after hiring him I sat down with Sankara and talked about that first day. He said, "I'll never forget it. I fell in love with the company upon arrival."

For many employees, the first day is a nerve-racking experience, and the anxiety only builds as they wait for someone to notice them. Sadly, for some, the first day can leave them feeling "dead on arrival."

My oldest son, Tyler, took a job at an environmental company. The owner is the type of person the phrase "he's good people" was written for, a truly awesome guy. The job, though, was far from awesome. On Tyler's first day, everyone was so busy putting out fires, he was ignored. When they finally took him on a project, they ended up asking him to work three hours of overtime. Then they left him alone to "monitor" the work on a project he knew nothing about, in a place he'd never been, with no way to communicate—until 9 p.m.

When Tyler returned home that night, after a fourteen-hour day, his fiancée asked him, "How was your first day?"

His response: "It sucked." One of the many phrases that indicates an employee's potential love for a company is dead on arrival.

Tyler went on to explain the events of the day and how it made him feel overwhelmed, disorganized, and ultimately, abandoned. His third day on the job, he gave his two-week notice.

There are two days you will surely remember for every job you have—the first and the last. You may not remember the details of the day's events. But you will remember how you felt. The reality is most people feel a version of disappointment on day one. So your job is to give a sense of joy, excitement, and anticipation at the start.

An employee's first day should be remarkable. When they are asked, "How was your first day?" their response should be, "Amazing!" followed by an excited rundown of just how great the day was for them. To do that, position their first day as a welcome celebration. Here's how we onboard employees on their first day:

- Give them a welcome basket with some items they may need for their job and something personal to them. We include a company mug and small self-heating kettle, a bag of coffee and a tin of tea, a water jug, a mix of snacks, their new business cards, and something that's related to their personal hobbies or interests.

- The number one supporter/detractor of an employee's job is the person they go home to, so we also include a gift for them in the welcome basket. We add a note that reads "We know (employee's name) decision to join our team is a significant one. We appreciate your support in their work with us. We hope you enjoy this gift." We choose a specific gift based on what we've learned about them during the employee's interview.

- For a remote worker's first day, send the welcome basket to their home that day. And because they won't get the full in-person experience, make the experience particularly special (we include helium balloons in the box that float up when they open it).

- Make the entire day about the employee, not just their first hour.

- Set up icebreakers with the team so they can get to know each other.

- Schedule a tour of the office with the boss, or a meeting with the boss, or both.

- Have a "welcome" lunch with everyone in the office. For remote workers, send lunch to their home and meet over video conference.

- Include your new employee in all regular office group activities.

- Introduce them to the huddle format (see below).

- Schedule their weekly one-on-ones (see p. 135).

HUDDLES

Ever watch a football game? Before most plays, the teams huddle. In one quick communication, the master plan for the next play is outlined. Sure, dynamics happen. Audibles are called. But each play is called out before it happens. Imagine if it didn't.

Imagine if the plan was simply, "Let's score a touchdown." How would the team ever be able to work in synchronization? Everyone would try their best, but without knowing the plan, they would not work in concert and might unintentionally hurt the team's progress. And imagine if a football team simply said, "We intend to win the Super Bowl this year." Sounds great, but what does the team need to do right now, in this next moment, to move toward that goal?

Business is the same. You have a team. You have goals for your company, department, and/or team. People know their role and how they are expected to block, tackle, and move the ball forward. But do they know what everyone else is doing for the next play? They should. The huddle is the fastest and most effective way to ensure that each team member knows what the team is doing as a whole, in that moment.

Huddles are daily group meetings, no longer than fifteen minutes. They are a great format for rapid sharing of corporate information. They are also an effective tool to help employees stay on track, and to foster togetherness. In a huddle, the group shares quick updates. For a team of fifteen employees or less, each person can get thirty seconds. For larger teams, you can have everyone attend and the department heads give updates, while inviting anyone else to share special announcements (such as birthdays, social activities, etc.). Or you may have many individual small team huddles and then immediately follow with a second one with the entire team.

Here's how we run our huddles:

- **We start at 9:01 every morning and are done by 9:16.** Time specificity encourages punctuality and efficiency. I found a 9:00 a.m. start was interpreted as 9:00 a.m.–ish, and 9:01 a.m. meant 9:01 a.m. And a "we run for fifteen minutes" goes on for far more than fifteen minutes.

- **Metric reports.** These are the key number updates on how we are doing in four main areas, the ACDC framework: Attracting customers, Converting prospects into clients, Delivering the promised offering to clients, and Collecting payment in return. We also report on the Queen Bee Role (QBR), the core function of the company that our success hinges on. (If you want to explore this further, the ACDC framework and the QBR are detailed in *Clockwork, Revised and Expanded: Design Your Business to Run Itself.*)

- **Yesterday's wins.** This is reserved for a big-deal win, such as landing a contract, deploying a new system, or raves from clients.

- **Red flags.** This is where we bring up any challenges or roadblocks, big or small. During one huddle at my forensics company, several people reported having internet connectivity issues. Because so many people shared the same red flag, we realized it was a network issue, not a PC issue. Sankara, who was still handling IT at the time, was able to fix the problem in minutes. Had the group not shared red flags, he would have had to try take time to determine that the problem was *not* a PC issue.

- **Shout-outs!** This is where we recognize fellow team members we spotted doing something helpful to move the organization forward.

- **Individual reports or department reports.** These updates are no longer than thirty seconds. Yes, you can present this stuff in thirty seconds. It is up to the huddle leader to move things along. Each person shares:

  » Big one from yesterday: What did you commit to? Was it completed? If not, how will it be addressed (e.g., no longer relevant, rescheduled, transferred to someone else, etc.)?

» Big one for today: What do you commit to for today?

» Personal update: One thing that happened in your life, big or small, since the last huddle.

■ **Prize wheel.** Based on your own criteria, have a way to recognize individuals and get a prize. For example, the person with the most shout-outs for the day gets to spin the prize wheel.

■ **Closing ritual.** Ever notice that a football huddle usually ends with a clap in unison? It is a simple way to bring conclusion to the brief meeting. Everyone knows the huddle is over and it is time for them to get into position for the play. At your office, end with a huddle-closing ritual. You could do a unison clap. You can have an empowering phrase everyone shouts out. Or, as we currently do, you could crank up the sounds of a pump-me-up tune as the team returns (sometimes dancing) to their work.

WEEKLY ONE-ON-ONES

Of all the retention tools in this chapter, the weekly one-on-ones have proven to be the most important. Kelsey Ayres, our president, said to me, "Our one-on-ones are the greatest thing we do for the team. It's what our employees look forward to the most, and it's even more effective than the group activities."

Months prior to the global pandemic, we had a plan to roll out one-on-ones during the following fall. But things changed when we were all forced to work remotely. Kelsey quickly implemented the one-on-ones to get a pulse on each employee. Because they had to meet over video conference, and Kelsey couldn't simply have an open-door policy for a check-in, she had to schedule the one-on-ones. Scheduling turned out to be a key factor in the success of this tool. Since employees know the time they'll meet with Kelsey each week, their job and their contentment is top of mind—for them, and for Kelsey.

Because every employee is heard, every week, we haven't had one instance that required a written "you need to fix this within fifteen days, or else" warning. We haven't had any problems that brewed for months and then blew up. No one has had to wait around for an annual review to discuss growth opportunities, expectations, or needs. Nothing waits. Everything—and I do mean every little thing—is addressed in the one-on-ones. This allows us to make simple course corrections. Not only can we address challenges right away, we can also spring on opportunities faster. Overall, there is greater connection at our company and more cohesiveness in our team.

You may be thinking, "Isn't this 'death by meetings'? Should I spend that time getting more of my work done, and allowing my team to get more of their work done?" This isn't about doing more work. The one-on-one is how you ensure the *right* work is getting done, and therefore *improves* efficiency.

Each one-one-one is scheduled for thirty minutes, though sometimes the meeting is over in ten minutes. Most of the conversation is just that—a conversation.

Here's the loose structure for one-on-ones:

- The first question should always be, "How are *you* doing?"
  The objective is to check in with the person first, not the job.

- An alternative question to ask, as shared in *The Coaching Habit* by Michael Bungay Stanier, is, "What's on your mind?" This question gives your colleague the opportunity to prioritize what is important to them. Because what is most important to them is most important to you.

- Then, discuss the work they are doing and their progress.

- Next, ask them if they are hitting any roadblocks. Not just on-the-job stuff, but anything they want to share that could be impeding them. For example, in my one-on-one, Kelsey asked me how I was doing with writing this book specifically. I explained my emotional struggle with my aging father's impending death. I wanted peace for him, and, selfishly, was afraid of the work that would instantly be on my plate when he passed away. Our conversations are full of humanness. Not just the comfortable. Not just the transactional.

- Then, discuss any areas that need correction and/or assistance. That is exactly what happened in that one-on-one. A solution presented itself: preplan for the funeral (yes, you can do this), implement power-of-attorney authorization before it is needed (yes, you can do that too). And my gosh, I was able to chip away at work and reduce my stress, so that when the inevitable happened, I didn't get overwhelmed with my family priorities *or* writing this book.

- Document actions and commitments and summarize. My favorite "trick" is that Kelsey has each person email her a summary of the meeting. The benefit is threefold. First, it reduces Kelsey's workload. Second, the person typing it up takes more ownership in what was discussed, because it is written in their own words. Third, it is empowering to be the person summarizing your own plan and adding tweaks or ideas as you ponder the discussion.

You can add components to your one-on-ones to suit your needs. Steve Bousquet, who you'll remember from the wheelbarrow story in chapter 6, also values the one-on-ones with his employees over all other tools. It is in these meetings that Steve learns about the seemingly small challenges his landscape crew has. This resulted in changes that not only solved the problem but also fostered psychological ownership *and* saved the company money.

When I asked Steve what questions he asks in his one-one-ones, he said, "What positive conversation or experience did you have in the company in the last week? What are you curious about? What questions have you been asking yourself, such as 'Should I be doing this?,' or 'Is this the right thing?,' or 'Is this better?'" With these questions, Steve can engage his employees in conversation about what is working and what they might need help with, and then come up with solutions.

QUARTERLY ONE-DAY RETREATS

I look forward to a few holidays in particular: July Fourth, Labor Day, Thanksgiving, and New Year's Eve. Yes, I have some specific rituals and family routines on those days. But the greater reason for my appreciation is that they trigger a disruption to work. Not only do I take off, but so do my employees and most of the people we serve in the United States. It is a time to rest a bit and reflect a bit.

And since I celebrate those days away from my workspaces, when I think about work, I think about it differently.

For our office we have a quarterly retreat. The idea is to intentionally disrupt ourselves from our repetitive work habits and look at our work another way. Don't get me wrong, our retreats are very much about work, just in a different type of way. We use them to tack our company and to tack ourselves.

Tacking is a strategy I originally wrote about in my first book, *The Toilet Paper Entrepreneur.* It is a term I took from sailors. Sailboats don't typically go in a straight line to their destination. Instead, they follow an alternating path. So instead of beelining your sailboat from the dock to that distant island, you zigzag your way there. That's tacking. You raise your sails and move in the general direction of that island, but in a way that captures the winds and avoids the obstacles. That's the zig. Then after a short distance, you turn the boat in a new direction, capturing winds, avoiding the new obstacles. That's the zag.

We tack our business every quarter by taking the optimal *short-term* path that captures the winds (of the economy, customer demand, etc.) and avoids the obstacles (of competition, product churn, etc.). You do this quarterly planning by removing yourself from day-to-day operations, just for a moment. This is your chance to realign your ship and adjust your sails (and, often, your sales).

The intention for retreats is twofold:

1. Provide an opportunity for team bonding to foster memorable experiences and time to connect. Human growth.

2. Leverage our time away from the office to brainstorm together, discuss current projects and challenges, and create action plans. Business growth.

At our quarterly meetings we work on realigning both the business and personal progress. Business elements include:

- A quarterly metric review.

- What were our goals from the prior quarter? What worked and what didn't? Tip: Always back your conclusions with the data, not hunches.

- What is not working or not working as well as intended in the business? How can we fix it? Should we abandon it?

- What is working? How can we amplify it? Or leverage it?

- What goals have changed and why?

Personal elements include:

- What is your progress on your individual goals?

- Where are you stuck and why? Where have you made progress and why?

- What goals have changed and why?

We often kick off the event with a team-building exercise, such as an obstacle course that required us to weave between paper cup lanes set up in a driveway. And we do some social stuff too: a meal together, a tour of another business, or something fun like roller skating or bowling. And sometimes something that turns out to be not fun at all, roller bowling.

We almost always schedule time for brainstorming at our quarterly retreats. This is where we may create new product ideas. For example, my first children's book came out of a brainstorm. We also might do mini projects, like sending out a bunch of thank-you videos from our team to key clients.

ANNUAL RETREATS

Kelsey has transformed our business into a community that is connected, empowered, and supportive—all the good stuff you want in a team. When an employee feels they are not just part of a company, but a community, they become more invested in their work and stay longer in their job.

Quarterly retreats go a long way toward building community. Our annual retreats, designed and led by Kelsey, are a game changer. The intentions are the same (see above), but the annual retreats offer a greater opportunity to connect. This is because our entire team is together for three days, including overnight. Kelsey explains, "When we are away, it allows everyone—the person who sits next to you, the person across the office, the people who work remotely—to have those little conversations that spark friendships. And, if nothing else, gain a better understanding of each other, which gives a level of humanity to every person who works with us."

At our annual retreats, we have more time to do creative brainstorming, and to do it in a way that fosters collective psychological ownership. Kelsey says, "We get everyone's input on potential ways to do things, and some great ideas have come out of that. The process makes everybody feel they have a stake in new initiatives, and the company overall." At past retreats we've come up with new products and offerings, different types of social media campaigns, and marketing ideas for book launches.

Annual retreats follow the same format as the quarterly retreats, with more time spent bonding, brainstorming, and then coming up with an action plan once we've decided on our most favorite or feasible option. We also engage in topical discussions and mini trainings, such as taking personality assessments, learning time management techniques, and going over our company goals and vision.

On my retired podcast, *Entrepreneurship Elevated*, Kelsey and I had the opportunity to interview Jon Berghoff, creator of the XCHANGE Approach. Jon is a group facilitation expert for leaders, and has led events for major companies such as BMW and Facebook. He explained that the first thirty minutes of any retreat should be focused on crowdsourcing the purpose of being "in the room."

Here is the process he shared:

1. First, each person answers the following questions:

    a. Why is it that our coming together to collectively shape our future is important?

    b. Why is this important to me?

    c. Why is this important to us?

    d. Why is this important to everyone who is not in the room (e.g., our families, our customers, our communities)?

2. Next, break into groups of three or four and share your answers with each other for ten minutes.

3. For the next ten minutes, each group will use posterboard and markers to create a presentation that answers the question, Why are we here?

4. Then, each small group delivers a shared purpose statement, ten words or less, and an image that embodies the essence of everyone's answers.

Jon explained that after the presentation, they decorate the walls with the posters, which remain up for the rest of the event.

He also recommended asking three additional questions during the retreat:

1. What's been working?

2. A year from now, what do we want to be celebrating?

3. What will we commit to—individually and collectively— to convert these images of what we want into committed actions?

However you design your annual retreat, make time to acknowledge each employee's wins. Celebrate their significant events, including those of their loved ones. Take time to know them as human beings. The bonds you forge at annual retreats will carry forward throughout the year and build a strong, tight-knit community.

ANNUAL REVIEW

After one year on the job, you should have had upward of forty one-on-ones with your employee, taking into account potential scheduling conflicts and vacations for your employee (and you). This means you won't have any surprises in this meeting. It doesn't have to be something your team dreads, like being called into the principal's office. And it doesn't have to be something *you* dread, either, because you have to talk about something you've been putting off. That's the beauty of the one-on-ones—you're not putting anything off. You know your employee well, you've course-corrected and handled challenges along the way, so there's nothing awkward about the meeting.

So, what's different about the annual review? It is a celebration of an employee's loyalty to the company. At the end of their lives, most people will have about fifty years of full-time work. Every year with you is one-fiftieth of their work life devoted to you. That is a big deal. Shoot, every five-year anniversary is a 10 percent chunk of their work life that was granted for you. It is an opportunity to re-celebrate. Just like we celebrate birthdays and anniversaries at home, this is their birth-a-versary at your company.

For most companies, the annual review coincides with a salary review. It doesn't need to be, but I suggest that you *do* a salary review and adjustment at this time. Salary isn't just recognition and compensation for people's contribution, it is also the budgeting for the company's financials. An alternative is to do all salary adjustments at the beginning of your fiscal year (ours is the same as the calendar year). This makes it even easier to budget and prepare.

The annual review is also the time to reconnect to an employee's potential. Nurturing the promise you saw in them in the hiring stage is an ongoing process. Use this yearly meeting as an opportunity to highlight their potential, what you saw in them when you hired them and how your view of them has expanded since. As people grow into their potential, their perspective shifts. What they once thought impossible may now seem doable. And what they once could not even imagine may seem possible. Does your employee want—or need—a new North Star? Are they demonstrating curiosity, desire, or thirst in new areas? Is there a better position for them to be in at your organization?

GOOD AND GREAT LEADERSHIP

Good Leaders	Great Leaders
Get Employees Up to Speed on the First Day The most common experience for new employees is "blah." They are quickly just put into the job without an opportunity to understand the business or meet the people. Good leaders ensure that their new employees have all they need to get started.	***Give Employees a Remarkable First Day*** The first impression is the biggest impression. Get it wrong and new employees will be disconnected from the start. Get it right and they will know you are all in for them. Great leaders celebrate the arrival of new employees.
Conduct Annual Reviews Meeting with employees to discuss their salary and performance is a corporate tradition. Good leaders also incorporate employee growth into the meeting.	***Meet with Employees Weekly*** When we have a good sense of how our employees are doing—both personally and professionally—we can get in front of challenges and course-correct as needed. Great leaders also meet one-on-one weekly with employees.
Hold Long Meetings Long meetings are helpful when you need to get everyone on the same page. Good leaders schedule meetings to solve big challenges and brainstorm new initiatives.	***Hold Daily Huddles*** Building team connection and unity requires regular group check-ins. Great leaders hold short, daily huddles that allow the team to sync up on the day.
Emphasize Team-Building Activities Team-building exercises as an isolated activity can seem contrived and not build much team bonding. But as part of a greater collective of activities they can be a good tool. The goal is to get many diverse activities. Have people spend time together in different ways at different times.	***Emphasize Unique Shared Experiences*** The goal for "team building" is to bond the group. The strongest bonds will trigger "remember when" stories among colleagues. "Remember whens" constitute shared, unique experiences and are anchors of strong relationships. Great leaders intentionally create bonding experiences that come from quality and quantity time. The goal is simple: build collective stories among the team.

8

Master the Ultimate
Motivational Tool

As thirty employees file into our small conference room, I cue up "Eye of the Tiger," Survivor's rock anthem written for the boxing movie *Rocky III*. The building guitar riffs that provided the soundtrack for Rocky Balboa's training montage fill the room, and I'm about to jump out of my skin.

Today is the day!

The announcement I'm about to make will be part of our company lore.

Those who are gathered here will remember this day for years—nah, decades—to come.

The first two years of our data forensics company, we experienced lightning in the bottle–type growth, at least for a bootstrapped business. My partner and I didn't put a penny into it, and the first year we had more than $600,000 in revenue. The second year, we achieved $3 million. And now, in year three, it was clear to me that we could hit $10 million. Ten. Million. Dollars.

All we needed was the right customer here, the right project there, and we would do it. So I spent the entire day in my office considering different iterations of the path forward. If we market to that kind of prospect. If we manage this type of project. If we hire that type of person. No, wait—if we market to *this* type of prospect, for *that* type of project, without any new people, we could do it. Yup. That's it. That's a lot of ifs—three, to be exact. But if we can get all three ifs in line, it was realistic that we would pass $10 million in revenue. I had never achieved that before and now it was within my grasp.

The hours of calculations and looking at historical data paid off. I had a clear path for significant growth.

I was convinced hitting $10 million in revenue in year three, in a sexy industry—investigating computer crime—was sure to get us on the cover of some magazine. The achievement would give us (cough, me) bragging rights. I just need everyone all in with me. So I planned the big announcement for the team. Drama, anticipation, a badass rock anthem. Then I called for this "all hands" meeting.

Our conference room fit twenty people comfortably, so with thirty employees, the room felt like a crowded bar. Once everyone settled in, I quieted the chitter-chatter with the classic "humble" power move: prayer hands to the chest, softly bite the lower lip, look each person in the eye as I nod my head, so everyone knows a big-ass announcement is coming.

"I'm proud of us. We've done amazing things. We have changed the industry"—dramatic pause, faux emotion, then drop the big line—"but we are just getting started." I said it slowly and powerfully, like a late-night DJ. I expected a minor roar from the team, or applause. Nothing yet, but I moved on unabated. They were about to lose their minds.

I turned to my temporary "metrics board," a whiteboard on which I stuck a giant Post-it. "I have been analyzing our trends, and I can see our future. I've discovered something big . . ."

I again paused for dramatic effect, timing it perfectly for the part of "Eye of the Tiger" when you see Rocky doing one-arm push-ups, hitting rocks with sledgehammers, standing on top of a mountain with his arms raised in a V.

Then, at just the right moment, I ripped off the Post-it to reveal the big goal number in black magic marker. In huge text I had written "$10M."

Like a boxer when they win an impossible match and rip the microphone out of the judge's hand, I yelled, "We are going to do ten million this year!"

When I visualized the moment, this is when everyone lost their shit. I imagined cheers, high-fives, even hugs.

Instead—crickets.

I felt as though I was Rocky on the steps of the Philadelphia Museum of Art throwing my arms up in victory—except I got pantsed, sweaty trousers hugging my ankles and tighty-whities exposed.

After a too-long, painfully awkward pause, I mumbled something about closing the meeting and everyone shuffled back to their normal work routine. Everyone except Patty Zanelli.

"Mike," she said, "when we do ten million, you get the new house and the new car. But what about us? Why should we care? That serves your dream. Not mine. Not theirs."

Ouch. I sat down in the nearest chair, feeling as though Ivan Drago, the Russian boxer in *Rocky IV*, had punched me dead center in the gut. I could barely breathe. Oh, the wisdom, the painful, painful wisdom. Patty was spot on. I was so caught up in my own dream, I didn't even consider how my team would feel about it. I just assumed they would be as psyched as I was.

The "corporate vision" is the owners' dream. But why should our employees care as much about achieving that dream as we do? They have their own dreams.

As leaders, we tend to get wrapped up in our own ideas. We can't expect enthusiasm for our dreams if we don't have enthusiasm for our employees' dreams.

Great leaders track each team member's personal dream and align their company's dream in such a way that everyone gets what they want. The company goals may not line up perfectly, but by simply knowing, supporting, and celebrating your team's dreams, they will, in turn, support and celebrate your company's dream. This is the ultimate motivational strategy.

Half our lives and most of our fullest energy is spent at work. The workplace must be a joyous place, a place where we can realize our full potential. Work is the greatest opportunity for us to be us, and our job as leaders is to help our team make the most of that opportunity.

THE JOY FORMULA

Paddy Condon had his own "Eye of the Tiger" moment, though he didn't have my dorky-dramatic flair. Owner of FBC Remodel, a design-build company operating in Colorado, Illinois, and Minnesota, he was always driving toward higher growth. In 2018, after a record $17 million year, he set a $20 million growth goal, and announced it at his company's annual meeting. Then he engaged his team to come up with a way to reach that goal.

"Designers and project managers don't get excited about top-line revenue goals," Paddy explained. "We needed to come up with a way to package the new goal so they would get behind it."

They kicked around ideas and came up with one that the entire team could really get around: two hundred happy homeowners. "We started talking about that," Paddy said, "but in reality, we were really just trying to drive revenue growth, and people can see that. People are smart."

That's when Paddy received some feedback that would prove to be life changing. The design leader in their Minneapolis office, Lyndsay Bussler, said, "I'm tired of going back to my team and saying, 'Hey, great job last year. Next year we want you to do 20 percent more.'"

"I didn't say anything," Paddy said, "but in my head I'm like, 'You're on my sales team, get behind this.' That's when Lyndsay said, 'You know, I just want to bring the team more joy.' Oh my God. It truly felt like one of those moments as a leader that happen maybe once every three years, when you are at a turning point and have to make a critical decision."

Paddy saw this moment as an opportunity to go all in on caring for his team. He looked up the definition of "joy" on his phone and noted that joy is "present when one experiences success and well-being. "I thought, 'Oh man, we've got the success side, that's the business. We need to support people in their well-being.'"

That's when Paddy created his original formula: success + well-being = joy. To implement the Joy Formula, Paddy and his team came up with a scorecard that tracked success and well-being. The success part was easy; they already had business metrics for the company as a whole and for each person's Primary Job. For the well-being scorecard, they came up with the "seven Fs": family, friends, fitness, faith, fun, finance, and forward (as in, What are you doing to move your life forward?). Every month, leaders meet with employees for a scorecard review. To prepare for that review, they've built a framework to help the team stay on track. That framework includes accountability groups and other support mechanisms.

What they discovered is that 70 percent of the scorecard review time is spent focusing on well-being. As Paddy explained it, "Well-being drives success. If a person is falling short or struggling with their seven Fs, it affects their job performance, because they are preoccupied, or stressed, or their mind is cluttered."

Despite a downturn in 2020 due to the pandemic, the following year FBC Remodel *surpassed* Paddy's $20 million revenue goal—they hit $25 million. Their close rates were up, and they became more efficient, which translated to a 50 percent increase in profit. Mind-boggling numbers, and in a very short time. They also retained their really good people, the people they wanted to keep; and the people they didn't want exited "really flipping quick."

Paddy said, "When people take ownership of their lives, they are ready to take ownership of your business."

The Joy Formula evolved to add purpose, because, as he discovered, when you add purpose "you've got a rocket ship." By connecting to their own purpose, employees are better able to connect to the company's purpose and goals. Here's the current version of the Joy Formula: (success + well-being) × purpose = joy. Purpose is the individual's vision for their life and their strategic plan to manifest that vision.

Adopting and committing to the Joy Formula changed Paddy's

perspective about, well, just about everything. Now he doesn't consider himself to be in the home remodeling or construction business. He considers himself to be in the human development business. "At the end of the day, you need your people to grow in their capabilities and mindset," he said. "If you don't grow your employees, you have to find them in the market."

Where Paddy was once all in on revenue growth, he is now all in on developing his team, on joy, and, as he puts it, "all in on love." And the revenue seemed to take care of itself. But you and I know it was actually his team that pulled it off. When Paddy focused on his team's dreams, they aligned themselves with the company's dreams and made them come true.

CARING ABOUT YOUR EMPLOYEES' DREAMS INSPIRES LOYALTY

Mary and Tony Miller had a people problem. In 1995, their Ohio-based janitorial services business, Jancoa, was struggling with employee turnover, absenteeism, and other staffing issues that cost them clients. If they couldn't solve their recruiting and retention challenges, they would forever be a struggling company at best or out of business at worst.

"We counted 104 cleaning companies in the greater Cincinnati area," Mary told me when I interviewed her for this book. "And we asked ourselves, 'With all the options job candidates have, why would they work for Jancoa?' We made a list of why people would want to work for us so we could attract more people."

Mary and Tony started to think of applicants and employees the same way they thought of customers. "We transferred the question 'What would we have to do to be a vendor of choice?' to 'What would we have to do to be an employer of choice?' We started thinking about how we could create value for our employees, and how we could help them overcome obstacles in their lives and have what they want."

Today, fifty years after they started Jancoa, they are the industry leader in the tri-state Cincinnati-area commercial cleaning market. They employ approximately five hundred loyal people. In an industry where employee turnover is the norm, their teams stay in the job longer *and* recruit others to join—more than 80 percent of new hires come from employee referrals.

Jancoa implemented several strategies to improve employee recruitment, retention, and performance, and the one that made the biggest difference was their Dream Engineer program. Made famous in the book by Matthew Kelly, *The Dream Manager*, the program evolved from Mary and Tony's efforts to help their employees realize their dreams. In individual meetings and group workshops, they helped their employees "think forward" and identify something they wanted to work toward. Then they helped them take steps to make their dreams a reality. Many employees dreamed of owning a home, for example, and Jancoa connected them with existing services and programs in their community to make that happen.

Through Mary, I had the opportunity to talk with one of their top-performing employees, Darryl Mason, who has worked for them for more than forty years. Through their Dream Engineer program, Darryl worked through debt and tax issues, learned how to budget, and eventually bought his own home. When I spoke with him, he kept referring to Jancoa as "my company," and client offices as "my buildings." By helping him imagine and then create a better life, Mary and Tony had instilled a strong sense of psychological ownership in Darryl. "They make you believe in yourself," Darryl explained.

The critical lesson in Jancoa's Dream Engineer program is that they prioritized their employees' dreams. However, they did not *give* them the dream. "Over-gifting" can give employees a sense of entitlement and diminish the value of the gift. Instead, Jancoa supported their employees in achieving their dreams; they gave them guidance, helped them find and utilize resources, and kept their dreams alive through regular check-ins.

"No one dreams of being a janitor," Mary said. Understanding this and supporting people in the discovery and pursuit of their dreams was the beginning of a new "culture of caring" at Jancoa. That culture inspired Kelly to write *The Dream Manager*, and Mary's own book, *Changing Direction: 10 Choices That Impact Your Dreams*.

It's true—no one dreams of being a janitor. But we *all* dream of "one day." One day I will visit Paris. One day I will learn to play the piano. One day I'll plant a vegetable garden. One day I'll get my college degree.

When you tap into your employees' dreams, their "one days," you show them you care about their whole potential—not just their potential to be a top performer for your company, but their potential to be truly fulfilled in life. By aligning your efforts for their dreams, you inspire them to align their efforts for your company's dreams.

Talking with Mary and Darryl reminded me of a famous story about a conversation then president John F. Kennedy had with a janitor at NASA in 1962. No one can confirm this story or knows the name of the man, but legend has it, Kennedy took a wrong turn down a hallway and ran into the janitor, who was carrying a broom.

Kennedy asked, "What are you doing?"

The janitor replied, "Mr. President, I'm helping put a man on the moon."

Yup. He sure was.

START WITH GOALS

Here's a question, and I want you to respond instantly: What's your dream?

I put you on the spot, I know. Maybe you had a thoughtful answer, but if you're like most people, you need some time to ruminate first. Some people blurt out the first "lifestyle improvement" that comes to mind—a bigger home, a newer car, a better vacation. Others can't wrap their head around how to answer at all. If dreams aren't considered deeply, repeatedly, they become nonexistent.

In chapter 3, I introduced you to Andrew Borg, the owner of a small manufacturing business who found high-potential employees at a trade school. He wanted to get to know his employees' dreams and help them achieve them. Yet most of his team had a version of a non-dream. Common non-dream indicators are "I just wants lots of money" or "I dunno."

When Andrew asked one of his employees to give vivid details on his dream, the dude rolled his eyes and said, "I just want to go home and have a beer, man." They were focused on getting through life, and rarely, if ever, expressed anything meaningful.

I mentioned this example to Mary Miller when I interviewed her. Since the release of *The Dream Manager*, she's met with numerous business owners and managers who struggle to get their own dream-focused program off the ground because employees don't seem interested. She explained that the program is not "plug and play" and that the culture of caring comes first.

"People have forgotten how to dream," Mary said. "You can't give up on them. Don't accept the surface responses and non-dreams. Stay present and have deeper conversations, so they know you really care."

Mary said when they first started the Dream Engineer program, they would ask about dreams during employee orientation. The number one response was, "I want to win the lottery." When they dug down deeper, when people felt safe to talk about their desires, when they felt heard, the dreams changed. "I remember one gentleman got really quiet, and then told the trainer, 'I want to learn how to read so I can read my daughter a bedtime story.' And so that's what we helped him work toward. And he realized that dream."

She went on to explain that dreams are different than goals, in that they are tied to strong personal emotions, and that those emotions mean possible pain. "If people have been through some stuff in their life and have different regrets, resentments, and disappointments, they're not going there. But for the most part, there are few emotions attached to goals, which are more task oriented. If goals are connected to a bigger dream, that's the way you can help people start dreaming again. And when you reintroduce people to their dreams, amazing things happen."

That's the barrier: the concept of a having a dream seems too big, too visionary, and we get emotional because it seems out of reach. We think of "movie" dreams, like qualifying for the Olympics, having a vacation home in the mountains, or becoming super wealthy. These dreams are not easily accessible because they require extraordinary effort and a big dose of luck. Even what seem like more doable dreams, like graduating from college or owning a home, can feel out of reach to some people, especially those who have been shaped by generational poverty. This is why we focus on intentions and goals, which are easier to wrap your head around. Sometimes those goals add up to a dream, and sometimes they don't. And sometimes the pursuit and achievement of a goal inspires people to start dreaming again.

Work with your team in a group session to identify their dreams. Some people may feel more comfortable talking about dreams in a one-on-one. Then work on breaking the dream down into a sequence of steps. Often the most effective way is to start with the dream and then work backwards on all the major steps. Find the starting point and support the team member in doing it. Publicly acknowledge and reinforce progress, no matter how small.

Caring about your team's goals shows them that you are all in for them. When you empower and organize the team around each other's goals, they are all in for each other. This is the ultimate motivator. For example, in one of our quarterly meetings, we talked about our "when I get around to it" plans that we never actually get around to. Cordé wanted an organized attic. Jeremy wanted a lift kit on his Jeep. I wanted a clean shed. We were all just a few steps away from fulfilling these doable goals, and yet they had lingered on our to-do lists for years.

So Kelsey responded with a "Do It Day." One day a year, we tie up the loose ends on our "doable" dreams. This is a paid day for the entire team. We meet over video conference to kick off the day and share our goals for the day that will have impact on us. Then we get to work on our individual projects. We check in throughout the day and report on our progress. Then we meet at the end of the day and give our final reports.

Cordé finally cleaned up her attic. Jeremy finally finished the work on his Jeep. And I finally took care of the shed. The feeling of accomplishment inspired all of us to think about bigger dreams we might go after. Beyond that, the appreciation for leadership's support has been huge. On multiple occasions since, Cordé has said, "I love that you guys helped me take care of my attic. I'm grateful to the company for helping me do something for me."

Another way to help your team identify their dreams is to ask them where they see themselves in three years, or five years. And sometimes, you just start with having a good day. What would it take to have one good day? If the answer is, "I just want to have a beer, man," then let's make that happen.

Never judge a dream. Dreams are in the eyes of the beholders. If it matters to them, it matters.

THE DREAM TREE

In our office in Boonton, New Jersey, you'll see a floor-to-ceiling tree on a wall near my office, covered in leaves with messages written on them. We call it the Dream Tree.

Every year, all our employees sit down with a big posterboard and markers and set their intentions and goals for the year. Sometimes they add dreams. Maybe they want to learn a new language, or have more family time, or play guitar, or work on their mental health.

Then everyone presents their poster to the group. We hang the posters up on the wall. Once a quarter, we review the posterboards. For every intention, goal, or dream achieved, we add a leaf to the Dream Tree. It is a great way to codify and publicly acknowledge our individual achievements.

We keep the posterboards up to help us stay on track but also to align with everyone's dreams. When the team knows what each individual wants for themselves, everyone can do their part to help them get it. Most of the time is spent cheerleading and keeping each other's dreams top of mind. Occasionally we offer direct support.

This reminds me of an anecdote Mary Miller shared with me. She said in a group meeting, one janitor mentioned that he wanted to take a class at a community college, but he couldn't do it because of his schedule. The class, which was more than half an hour's drive from his location, started at six o'clock, and he didn't get off until five-thirty. There was no way he could make it in time. One of his coworkers asked how long the class would last. When he learned it would be six weeks, he offered to temporarily switch shifts so his coworker could take the class.

The Dream Tree shows you are all in for your employees, and it helps them demonstrate they are all in for each other.

But you don't need a tree. You simply need to help your team envision what they want to do, achieve, or become, and then post that dream or goal in a common space. At FBC Remodel, Paddy's team creates a dream board with three-year and ten-year goals, and a personal vision tracker, and then posts it on their "dream wall."

They also come with a strategic plan to realize their vision and then track that plan in their monthly scorecard meetings. This initiative has had an unexpected benefit. After twenty years of trying to get his team to understand and rally behind the company's strategic plan, his efforts finally clicked. "When you teach them how to do a strategic plan for their life—purpose, measurable goals, all that—people who didn't have a clue how the company's strategic plan worked suddenly get it."

Paddy added, "And when their purpose aligns with your company's purpose, you know you're in the right spot." He shared an example of Kyle, who started out in an entry-level construction position, and as he worked his own strategic plan, he had a thirst to achieve the company's plan. Kyle quickly rose up the ranks to project manager.

"When you teach somebody how to own their life, they own all the results in their position," Paddy said. That translated to Kyle's laser focus on materials costs and cutting waste. Most project managers had losses of materials on job sites that totaled hundreds of thousands of dollars. Not Kyle. He saw the alignment between efficiency and cost control in his own life's goals and the goals of FBC Remodels. As a result, he saved the company $500,000 for each job site. Talk about psychological ownership!

However you implement it, focusing on your team's dreams pays numerous dividends—it's a no-brainer.

GOOD AND GREAT LEADERSHIP

Good Leaders	Great Leaders
Focus on Job Progression and Salaries Most employees want to move up in the company, and they want to be compensated for their growth and outcomes achieved. Good leaders know their employees' goals within the company and create a clear path to achieve them.	**Help Employees Set Goals and Dreams** Money and career advancement are important, but they are not the whole picture. Your team cares as much—or more—about their personal goals and dreams. Great leaders ask their team to express and document their dreams, however simple, and then guides them in achieving it.
Focus on Corporate Vision Focusing on what is urgent, rather than what is important, impedes progress and can lead to team burnout. When your employees know how and where you want your company to grow, they can see that their work matters. Good leaders create a strong company vision and communicate it to their team.	**Focus on the Collective Path** Zig Ziglar famously said, "If you help enough people get what they want, you will get what you want." When employees feel their individual goals matter as much as the company's goals, they are even more motivated to see that company goal come to fruition. Great leaders align their company vision with their employees' personal vision.
Reward Work Performance When an employee meets or exceeds your expectations, it's important to reward them for a job well done. Good leaders acknowledge and encourage their team's work performance and contribution.	**Reward Work-Life Balance** Work is a big part of people's lives. So make their lives a bigger part of work. Great leaders incorporate life updates into daily huddles, one-on-ones, and quarterly updates.

9

Build Community First

One of my favorite examples of an unstoppable team is the motley crew in *The Wizard of Oz*. The Scarecrow, the Tin Man, the Cowardly Lion, and Dorothy work cohesively to achieve their "corporate" mission: get to Oz. And their individual dreams—to get a brain, a heart, courage, and a one-way ticket home to Kansas—align with their collective goal. As they follow the yellow brick road, they are one-for-all and all-for-one; they care as much about each other's individual dreams as they do about their own.

There's no denying that this fictional team is unstoppable. They navigate sometimes treacherous terrain, survive being drugged by a field of poppies, defeat the Wicked Witch of the West, and confront the con man behind the curtain. And don't forget the terror of all terrors, the flying monkeys! In the end, they achieve their group and personal missions.

What I find fascinating about Dorothy and her new friends is that they are missing something we in the business world have decided is crucial for effective team building: culture. They don't have a set of shared values. Mission, yes. Values, not so much. They don't all share courage or heart. If you don't have smarts, you aren't off the yellow brick team. Everyone is in, even Toto.

What they do have is community. They are a diverse group of individuals who unify around a shared purpose. They are part of something bigger than their own circumstances and aims. And the community they've created gives them a sense of belonging and connection, which fortifies them. They are not alone in their quests.

If Dorothy had stayed in the land of Oz rather than head back to the farm, they might have developed a common culture around loyalty, honesty, kindness, optimism, and not leaving anyone behind. Yeah, I'm just spitballin' here based on how the characters handle themselves in the movie, but I'm probably not far off. And those values would come *from* the team, not from a higher source.

As leaders, we spend a lot of time thinking about culture and drafting our company values. We tend to focus on what matters to us and then enroll our employees in that culture. While company values, ideals, and policies matter a lot, this top-down approach does not work as well when teams do not *first* feel a sense of belonging. Culture fails because it is dogmatic, not diverse; it is words, not action.

Focusing on culture first can also result in a narrow focus, even when we have the best intentions. When culture is mandated from the big cheese, it may not resonate with your employees. By deciding your corporate values *for* your team rather than creating a culture that is *because of them*, you could be missing major contributions *from* your team.

If we want to create a culture born of community, we must first build community. It's through community that we strengthen and deepen connection. And any culture that comes from this place of belonging will mean far more than words. This is the inclusive approach. If you want to think about this philosophically: culture is "I am, so, we are," whereas community is "We are, so, we are."

If you've started implementing any of the ideas in this book, you're already building community. You provide a safe workplace where your employees can be their authentic selves. You have given them a sense of ownership over their job and the company's mission. You have systems in place to make them feel welcome and wanted from day one, and to foster connection throughout the year. You have taken an interest in their personal dreams, goals, and intentions. You've given them opportunities to grow and share in knowledge. You've created conditions in which each individual can thrive according to their interests and communication preferences.

And now, let's do more.

RESONANT WORKPLACE CULTURE IS BORN OF COMMUNITY

In chapter 5, I shared Rhodes Perry's story about psychological safety and working for the White House. When I asked him about building community versus culture, he said, "Culture is communicated from the top. It's a mandate. Community is morphic."

In biology, "morphic" is the naturally occurring shape or form of something. Community is the shape or form of the collective people who work at and with your company. The shape changes as people come and go, and as people grow. As our community changes (morphs), so should the things that define us. Although your personal values may never change, the communal values just might.

While I was in the process of writing this book, our company held our annual retreat. Since we were all together, I took the opportunity to get a read on our values, which I call Immutable Laws. Kelsey asked me to explain the values, and to my surprise, no one knew all of them. And those who did knew one or two, understood the words but had their own definition, or didn't really embrace them.

A good example of this is "No dicks allowed." I've held fast to that Immutable Law for decades. I wrote about it in my first book. It means just what you think it means—we don't work with people who exhibit dick-like behavior, and I don't accept dick-like behavior from myself (as I realized in that fateful moment when I was fired from Robert Half International). You may have a different word for the type of people who act like jerks. Oddly enough, many of them have a consistent dicklike meaning (e.g., prick, weenie, schmuck—I could go on).

In our office, we now have more women than men. When they heard me share "No dicks allowed," the response was, "That's bro-ey."

Yup. They were right. That Immutable Law, which had been set by me and gone unchanged for years, was definitely bro-ey. Though my team could get behind the meaning once I explained it, the phrasing turned them off. Yes, it is who *I* am, but collectively, that's not who *we* are. So we discussed it as a community and changed the phrasing to our common language, "Goodness is greatness." As the leader, I am an equal participant in the meaning behind our communal value. But the community—my team *and* me—came up with the value that fits us best.

I used to believe that Immutable Laws were defined by the first person on board, the founder or founding team, and that everyone who followed had to comply with the template. But the reality is, as our community grows and diversity is encouraged, bigger, perhaps more accepting values come about. Resonant workplace culture is born of community.

We started talking about other Immutable Laws and reinvented or refreshed them for our new community, our new shape. One was "Positivity or death." When I set that value, the meaning behind it was we need to focus on the good, or we will decline. My team noted that my phrasing didn't ring true. It seemed fake, too dramatic. Together, we came up with a new version that suits our community: "Be their Ted Lasso."

If you've never seen the Apple television series *Ted Lasso*, it's about an American football coach who is hired to coach a notably average and somewhat dysfunctional English Premier League "football" team. You know, a soccer team. Even though he doesn't know anything about the sport, he cares so much about the players and is so steadfast in his positive mindset that he turns the team into a true contender. That's what my company strives to do for our readers and clients. We care so much about them, and we want to be of service to them; it doesn't matter if we know much about their businesses. "Be their Ted Lasso" is a modernization of "Positivity or death," one that resonates with our community.

I want to note my own hypocrisy here. I defined Immutable Laws as just that—immutable, unchanging. But my research of great leaders and my experience developing and testing FASO challenged my steadfast belief. Diversity in your organization requires a refresh or redefinition of the collective values. As it turns out, Immutable Laws are not immutable at all. Just as laws change as society evolves, yours may evolve as your team community grows. The great poet Maya Angelou once said, "Do the best you can until you know better. Then when you know better, do better."

When you know better, do better.

IMMUTABLE LAWS

At the 1-800-GOT-JUNK? headquarters in Vancouver, British Columbia, with its founder, Brian Scudamore, I noticed an acronym posted boldly on the wall: PIPE. Whenever I'm touring a business, I'm like an excited kindergartner who's just learning to read, always naming signs out loud. I blurted, "Pipe!" Without looking at the wall, Brian said as if on cue, "Passion, integrity, professionalism, and empathy." He had memorized his company's values, which is to be expected of great leaders.

Does his team live by these Immutable Laws? Would his team be able to recite them? I wanted to find out.

As we made our way through the building, I asked every employee I met if they could tell me the 1-800-GOT-JUNK? company values. To my surprise and Brian's, none of them could remember all four, and some couldn't remember any of them. They walked by the walls, the signs, the reminders every day, and yet they couldn't remember them.

"I'm embarrassed," Brian said. "The values are what define this organization. But the fact our people didn't remember our values or even the acronym on the wall . . . well, I don't know what to say."

Brian's team shared a lot with me that day.

One person said, "I just love up on our customers. They are doing amazing things in their lives. They are bringing back order, taking control, or just sprucing up their place. No matter what it is, the fact that we are part of that journey is pretty darn awesome. That deserves all the love I've got."

Another person said, "Some of our clients are in a bad situation when they call us. Junk removal isn't always about cleaning up. Sometimes it is about getting out, like when they're getting a divorce.

Other times people are starting all over, like after a fire. This is more than a project; it is a change in someone's life."

And another team member shared, "I remember once we had a client junk tons of metal. Something they were just going to dump. Our team, behind the scenes, sorted through every scrap so that it could be recycled fully. I feel so good about that. We served the client and the planet."

Then, when we were near the end of our tour, we turned the corner into a large conference room. It was a few minutes before ten, and a large group of people had assembled for a meeting, which started on the hour.

"Early birds?" I asked, expecting that more people would show up at eleven, or a few minutes after.

Brian chuckled and said, "No. This is everyone. We all get here early so we can hit the ground running. It's the ultimate way to show respect for each other's most precious resource—time."

With one minute left before the meeting started, I turned to Brian and said, "Your employees may not be saying the words, but they are living the Immutable Laws. They get it. They more than get it; they have integrated it."

Brian's employees weren't repeating the PIPE acronym verbatim, but they were doing something more important: they were using their own words. The company values had become so ingrained in his team that they had made them their own.

What's better? Employees who memorize company values and don't embody them, or employees who may forget the specific words you used, but live and breathe those values every day?

Maybe 1-800-GOT-JUNK? could refresh the words on the wall so the team can recall them better. But, then again, it is not about words. It is about the embodiment of the collective Immutable Laws.

Everyone there had made the values their own, which is a level up from choice words. Brian and the leadership team lived the values, and as a result so did their entire community.

As I parted ways with Brian at the end of the day, he said, "I was so pleasantly surprised to see PIPE on the wall. Our team posted that. They came up with the wording and posted it. I committed to memorizing." Yes, and like you, Brian, they committed to living them, because it is how they already were living, collectively.

BELONGING IS A KEY COMPONENT OF COMMUNITY

Dorothy and her team used their abilities—experiential, innate, and potential—to solve problems, get past ornery gatekeepers, and rescue their friends. What if one of them felt they didn't belong in the group? Would they have had the same sense of community? Would they have had the diverse group of talents to pull off their mission? I think without all four—plus Toto—the story would have had a very different ending.

Belonging is a core human need. If you're not familiar with Abraham Maslow's hierarchy of needs, it is a model for understanding human motivation. The five categories—physiological needs, safety needs, belonging and love needs, esteem needs, and self-actualization needs—are tiered in a pyramid, in ascending order. Belonging and love needs are right there in the middle of the pyramid. This category sits above the two first needs: physiological and safety, the stuff we need to survive, like water, food, shelter, and security.

Without belonging, we can't have community. But how do we cultivate it? How do we make sure everyone on our team feels they belong?

Rhodes Perry wrote two books on the subject, *Imagine Belonging* and *Belonging at Work*. In our conversation, he said, "People ask, 'What is belonging in the workplace?' They think it's too elusive and can't be measured. Actually, you can."

According to Rhodes, to measure belonging, it comes down to four elements, which come from a study created by Coqual, formerly the Center for Talent and Innovation:

1. Feeling seen—showing up fully as who you are, all the genius you bring into the workplace, and all your lived experience.

2. Feeling connected—having authentic relationships with your colleagues, where you can share as much as you want about yourself, and when you do, they will receive it with care.

3. Feeling supported—people have your back and you get what you need so you can do your best work.

4. Feeling pride—when your own values and purpose complement the organization you work within.

"When you have all four elements, people are off to the races," Rhodes added. "Without those elements, you feel the inverse of belonging. So if you're not feeling seen, you feel invisible. If you're not feeling connected, you're feeling distant. If you're not getting support, you're feeling discouraged. If you're not feeling a sense of pride, then you're feeling shame. That's when you start to wonder, 'What about me doesn't align with this organization?' And that's when you are in a stress state and definitely not giving it your all. You're in protective mode, just trying to survive."

Tricia Montalvo Timm spent most of her career in protective mode. A corporate lawyer, she worked in Silicon Valley for twenty-five years. She loved helping companies scale from a few hundred employees to more than a thousand. As general counsel for Looker Data Sciences, she helped sell the company to Google for a $2.6 billion valuation. And yet despite her professional success, Tricia often felt she did not belong in her workplace. To fit in, she had been hiding her Latina identity since her early days in Silicon Valley. Ironically, the very thing she did to try to feel as though she belonged only made her feel more disconnected.

When I talked with Tricia, she told me, "I required a lot of myself to change, so I could fit in."

In her book *Embrace the Power of You: Owning Your Identity at Work*, Tricia shares a story about when she first "came out" about being Latina. It was during Hispanic Heritage Month, while at Looker, that she shared her identity with her boss. He encouraged her to tell her story to the entire company. At first she was reluctant, but then she found the courage and agreed. In front of hundreds of coworkers, she talked about her father, who is from Ecuador, and her mother, who is from El Salvador. She shared stories about trying to blend in with her white male coworkers. She talked about staying late at the office so she could speak Spanish with the janitor.

Sharing her story opened doors for Tricia's Hispanic colleagues to share their own stories, and for everyone on the team to show up authentically at work. She said, "When people hear the stories of their colleague sitting right next to them, whom they have worked with for five years and never realized their true lived experience—be it race, gender, sexual orientation, religion—it starts to create empathy."

Storytelling can be a lifeline for your team, one that ultimately strengthens your community. Tricia added, "People realize, 'Oh, I didn't know this dimensionality of who you are and this amazing experience you bring to the table.' Then, by sharing their story, that person now feels a better connection and can bring their fuller self to the workplace."

I'm pretty sure most of my employees have felt stifled at work at some point, and I know I have. To some extent, we all switch personas when we get to work and turn on our "real selves" when we pull out of the parking lot to head home. Do you know how exhausting that is, to keep pretending? Now imagine feeling that way about your identity, so much so that you hide fundamental parts of yourself.

I believe, to have a sense of belonging, a certain level of intimacy is required. I'm talking about the intimacy you have with close friends. The people you've chosen as "your people." You have inside jokes and shared experiences. You've celebrated with them, and you've mourned with them. You've been vulnerable with them; they've seen you at your best and at your worst. These relationships are built on caring and trust. It feels good just thinking about your peeps, doesn't it?

We need this same feeling at work. It's a delicate balance, creating intimacy while maintaining professionalism, but it can be done. I know because we've done this at our company. When intimacy is achieved, it elevates your work relationships and ultimately elevates your offering. And it is through these close relationships that you can truly see someone's potential. When a person feels they belong, when they feel safe to share who they really are—their interests, their passions, their challenges, their secret hopes—*you* can help them step into that potentiality. You might even help them explore their full potential and become who they were meant to be.

FOCUS ON INDIVIDUAL POTENTIAL
IMPROVES THE WHOLE

Daniel Eugene Ruettiger had a dream to play football for Notre Dame. You may know him by his nickname, Rudy, which is the title of the 1993 movie based on his story. What you may not know is that the movie bent the facts to suit their narrative. The true story is even more inspiring than the one portrayed in the film.

After serving in the Navy, Ruettiger applied to Notre Dame. He was rejected due to low grades, but after his fourth attempt in two years, he finally received his acceptance letter. At Notre Dame, he tried out for the football team, hoping to at least earn a walk-on spot. But Ruettiger was small in stature and didn't have the level of talent most college players had. While he did get onto the school's scout team, for three years he never made it onto the "dress roster," the Fighting Irish team that plays on Saturdays.

In the movie *Rudy*, Ruettiger asks the new coach, Dan Devine, if he can "dress" for the last home game, his last chance to finally realize his dream. Devine tells him no, and it's his teammates who change the coach's mind. The story shows a great team turning the heart of a curmudgeonly leader.

In real life, it was Devine's idea. He asked Rudy to dress for the last game. He remained close to Ruettiger after he graduated, and as a favor to him agreed to be painted as a villain in the movie so that it would be greenlit.

In reality, Devine saw potential in Ruettiger—not as a player, necessarily, but as a human being with a dream. And by honoring that dream, Devine demonstrated he was a great leader. His decision elevated Ruettiger, and it elevated the entire team.

Ruettiger was on the field for only three plays: a kickoff, an incomplete pass, and, in the final play, a sack. After the game, his teammates carried him off the field. He was the first player in Notre Dame's history to receive that honor—and only one player has received it since.

When someone goes all out on a dream, it elevates others to go all out on theirs. Ruettiger wasn't the star. For nearly all of his college career, he wasn't even a player. But my God, he was a contributor. Ruettiger was the motivational center of the team. By design, sports *is* community, but his spirit and Devine's commitment to potential strengthened their community.

Ruettiger had a powerful "affective appearance," a psychological term for how people see you and respond. Hillary Elfenbein, professor of organizational behavior at Olin Business School at Washington University in St. Louis, refers to this as an "emotional signature." The way we walk into a room is felt by others. The way you show up matters.

Ruettiger's teammate Jay Achterhoff said, "You've never in your life seen a guy who wanted to be on the field more." Ruettiger expected the most from himself. That emotional signature just may have further inspired his teammates to expect more from themselves. During his time on the team, Notre Dame ranked fourth in the nation (1974), seventeenth (1975), and twelfth, the same year they won the bowl championship (1976).

In the years after Ruettiger left, Notre Dame's football team started to struggle. Now, that could be attributed to any number of factors; there's no statistical proof of Ruettiger's impact on the team. But there is one piece of undeniable proof: he was the first person ever carried off the field in a game-winning celebration *by the team*. You decide if his efforts—and Devine's support—motivated them.

CULTURE IS STATIC, COMMUNITIES ARE ACTIVE

When the Westboro Baptist Church announced they were coming to Nyack High School in Nyack, New York, to protest a play, the community jumped into action. A hate group that picketed military funerals and other events, carrying signs with horrible messages to draw attention to their antigay views, Westboro objected to the play the students chose to put on that year, *The Laramie Project*. The play explored the reaction to the 1998 murder of Matthew Shepard, a gay University of Wyoming student.

A progressive community that included many gay and lesbian families, Nyackers did *not* want Westboro to step foot in their village, nor did they want them to disrupt the play. Almost immediately, an email campaign circulated asking neighbors to purchase tickets for the play so the hate group could not get a seat. Within hours, every performance was sold out.

Westboro Baptist Church did not come to Nyack to protest the play, or any other event.

What struck me when I heard this story was that most of the people who bought tickets were not a part of the LGBTQ+ community. And that no one had to remind anyone of their community values or make a speech about equality. When presented with what they perceived to be a threat to their community as a whole, they shut it down. And fast. "Not in my community, you don't" was the feeling—hello, psychological ownership (the O in FASO).

The beauty of fostering community in the workplace is it is dynamic and active. A community can organize quickly to solve known threats, to help others in need, to manage crises, and to solve problems. A community can also assemble quickly to celebrate victories, personal and professional—like a block party, right in the office. A community is stronger than the sum of its parts, the sum of each individual's potential. It is a shapeshifting, evolving, diverse, joyous, powerful force. And when you have a thriving community, your employees will not only want to stay in it, but they will also want to contribute to it again, and again, and again.

GOOD AND GREAT LEADERSHIP

Good Leaders	Great Leaders
Build Culture First Company culture brings about a narrow focus that unifies your team. Good leaders consider the Immutable Laws that are important to them and share those values with their team.	**Create Community First** When you create community first, culture is born of the community and reflects the whole. Great leaders implement Immutable Laws as a representation of the entirety of the organization.
Encourage Diversity A diverse team brings to an organization perspective and awareness to both opportunities and challenges. Good leaders welcome people of all types and backgrounds.	**Seek Diversity** Diversity doesn't happen by accident; a diverse team is built deliberately and thoughtfully. Great leaders actively seek diverse teams and create the systems to support them.

10

Up-Level Employee Experience
and Performance

My first job after college was with a computer retailer who provided tech services for businesses. My new position was programmer, the old-school term for coder. I didn't do that work for long, because through happenstance exposure to other work, they discovered I had stronger potential elsewhere. I could represent the company, I could sell computers, printers, and network projects, and I could teach. Very quickly I became a "rising star," in part because I was so young and driven.

At that company, I had a Bad Boss and a Good Boss. Bad Boss gave me my first assignment in my new sales role, to respond to a government bid. It was a fifty-page request for proposal (RFP), and the requirements were like nothing I'd ever seen before. I had to include details on every little thing, like the weight of the equipment and the manufacturing source of the nuts and bolts holding the machines together. I had one week to respond, so every day I did my regular duties and then stayed late into the night to work on the RFP, and then when the weekend arrived, I worked on the proposal for twelve hours on Saturday and twelve hours on Sunday.

When I turned in the RFP on time on Monday morning—printed and bound, no less—Bad Boss looked stupefied. He said, "We've never completed one of these bids before. They are overwhelming."

My chest swelled up with pride. I had accomplished something no one at my company had done before!

Bad Boss flipped through the pages of my hard work and sleepless nights and said, "Since we don't work with the government, even if we win the lottery and win this bid, we wouldn't know how to service it." He then dropped the proposal right into his garbage can—*thunk!* Then he chuckled and said, "I didn't think you would actually get it all done. Good job. Get back to work."

Dan Cable, professor of organizational behavior at London Business School, once said, "I wonder what my soul does all day when I'm at work?" It is the sad state of affairs for many workers, leaving our souls, our hearts, our joy behind for a job. That was certainly true for me in that moment. When I was doing work that was meaningless, I felt meaningless. I was assigned stuff just to make me work harder and longer. Maybe Bad Boss wanted to see if I would break due to his subterfuge.

Good job? I was so pissed. And sad. And confused. Bad Boss had given me a task, I went all in on it, and it was a joke to him? Psychological safety—destroyed. Psychological ownership—gone. The blatant disregard for my work by the exact person who gave me the task rocked me to my core, but I was determined to try to find my way at the company.

Still, Bad Boss made it hard to stick around. He was big on punishment, and he made a show of it. I remember one time I made a mistake while installing antivirus software for a client; I neglected to put the most current version on some of their machines. One of them got infected with a virus, and the client found out and called our office. For that mistake, Bad Boss made me apologize to the client, which was fine, and I was happy to do it. Then he ordered me to re-install the software on every machine *while he watched over my shoulder* to make sure I didn't "screw it up again." Lastly, Bad Boss made me sit in my cubicle for an entire day and read every word in the instruction manual, front to back—at least five times—and then write a report on it. And yet even after all that, I still wanted to prove that I was the best. Maybe I was trying to prove to myself I was un-breakable. Or maybe, just maybe, I stayed as long as I did because of Good Boss.

Good Boss was my immediate supervisor. He listened, engaged, and supported me. Rather than punish me for mistakes, he saw them as opportunities to help me grow. He'd call me into his office for a debrief to figure out how we could make improvements. He publicly acknowledged my successes, and those of other people on the team.

Good Boss saw potential in me and helped me identify new strengths and see new possibilities, which in turn helped the com-pany. He once told me, "You could be a suit here one day." That was his way of telling me I was a rising star, a future leader.

Good Boss was all about empowering people so we could depend on ourselves.

Bad Boss was all about intimidating people so we would depend on him.

For a time, Good Boss's efforts outweighed Bad Boss's behavior, until it didn't. I'd stopped caring about the company and spent a lot of nights complaining about Bad Boss into my beer. Finally, I said, "Why am I working for this guy, when I could be working for myself?"

One of the reasons I stayed at the company as long as I did, despite Bad Boss's ways, was because they trained me. It was all Good Boss's idea. He said, "Mike can teach Novell classes to our clients," and got me trained up. Novell was the main network operating system at the time. Good Boss even attended my first few classes with me so he could help me if I stumbled.* He also convinced Bad Boss to send me to Dale Carnegie courses, which were amazing, and to a Tony Robbins event. I loved these trainings and classes. They shaped me, and because I had a deep interest in learning and teaching, they helped me become the person I am today. Good Boss also cared about me as an individual. He knew I liked playing team sports and would come down to the basketball courts to play a game with me and fellow colleagues. No one was particularly good at basketball, but I loved the time we spent together shooting baskets and talking smack. Good Boss was present. No surprise, Bad Boss never was.

Good Boss cared about my experience working at the company, and he continually made efforts to improve that experience by giving *me opportunities to improve myself*. He noticed me, and tried to understand me, so he could better communicate with me. And rather than dominate me, he worked *with* me.

In my final week, Bad Boss looked at me and said, "You're a loose cannon, Michalowicz. If you would simply do what you're told, you could be successful."

Good Boss, who had been standing off to the side, walked up to us and, in front of Bad Boss (who was his boss too), said, "You're a

---

* Though I didn't realize it at the time, the Novell classes I taught were workshops. Many students simply learned how to manage Novell networks. But a few noticed how much we knew and became clients. And the best of the best—you guessed it—were invited to join our company as network engineers.

cannon for sure, Mike. I want to do everything I can to leverage your firepower. Thanks for being part of our team."

Please know that I am not saying Bad Boss is a bad person. I don't believe he had ill intent. I believe he, like me and you, is a product of his life's experiences. Maybe someone exerted control over him, or maybe he only got attention from family if he was assertive. I don't know. I am simply saying he is not a bad person, just a bad boss.

Bad Boss tried to control me. Good Boss tried to channel me. Bad leaders state their desires and try to make people comply. Great leaders encourage people to express their own desires and align them with the company's needs.

Part of being all in for our team is creating an environment that allows them to reach their potential. You're already doing that by implementing FASO and following the Retention Rhythm. With that in place, you're ready to implement three powerful strategies that will up-level your employee experience and, in turn, help your company grow.

Be the good boss.

STRATEGY #1: GIVE EMPLOYEES OPPORTUNITIES TO GROW

My wife, Krista, learned to read early, when she was four years old. She still recalls with excitement the moment she pointed at a sign on a building and said, "Kay . . . Kay . . . Kayma . . . Kaymard . . . Kaymart." Yes, the Kmart sign was my wife's first reading experience. (And she's been loyal to the store ever since.) Krista loves to tell this story because it's cute, sure, but also because she's proud of it.

Learning is at the core of self-esteem, personal and professional growth, and survival. One of the best ways we can up-level employee performance *and* help them reach their potential is to give them opportunities to grow and learn.

A study conducted by Umeå University in Sweden of fifteen thousand people across twenty-five countries found that the countries that supported ongoing education had happier citizens than those that didn't support education. People are happier when they learn, in countries and in companies.

Here's what learning does for your team:

1. Serves FASO. Learning equips them to serve their fit in the company better. Learning also expands their ability, can enable greater safety, and enhances ownership.

2. Fuels Maslow's hierarchy of needs:

   a. Safety: Relevance and skill to ensure they remain employable.

   b. Esteem: Self-esteem, respect, status, and freedom through growing in knowledge and demonstrable capability.

   c. Self-actualization: They reach their potential.

3. Grows the three key qualities—learn, listen, limber.

4. Sparks new ideas that can serve the company.

5. Helps employees stay ahead of the curve with the latest technology, trends, and strategies.

To be great leaders, we must teach, train, mentor, and guide our teams—either directly or through outside learning programs. Do you have any of the following in place?

- On-the-job training

- Apprenticeships/internships

- Rehearsals/role-playing

- Instructional training

- Interactive training

- Mentoring/coaching

- A combination of the above

If you don't have training opportunities in place for your team, where could you start? I weathered many screaming sessions and humiliating moments with my Bad Boss just so I could continue to learn (thanks to my Good Boss). Imagine what could have happened if that company had a system like FASO in place? I might have become one of the "suits," as Good Boss predicted. Heck, I might still be working there today.

I'm not the only person who felt that way. The *2022 Workplace Learning Report* study from LinkedIn identified that 94 percent of employees said they would stay at a company longer if the company simply invested in helping them learn. And yet I still hear business leaders say things like, "If you train your people, they may grow out of your company and leave." They also express fears about the financial costs. I get it—paying for classes and sometimes travel *to* the classes, plus their salary while they attend, seems like a risky endeavor. What if they take their newfound knowledge to one of your competitors? What if they expect a raise because now they have qualifications they didn't have when you hired them? What if—gulp—they end up knowing more about your business than you do?

If you train people, they may go. But if you don't, they will stay—stay in the job *and* stay at the same level. Neglecting to train your team is a surefire way to slowly fall further and further behind your competition.

I hope you can set aside those fears and focus on this: training your people makes them better, and it makes them like *you* better. In this way, providing learning opportunities is the ultimate gift.

STRATEGY #2: CREATE PERSONAL OPERATING MANUALS

"Why do people disconnect on expectations?" This was the question my friend Darren Virassammy, COO and cofounder of 34 Strong, asked me during one of our conversations about employee engagement. As leading experts in strengths-based development, employee engagement measurement, and consulting, 34 Strong's clients include multinational corporations such as Johnson & Johnson, Bank of America, and Microsoft.

"Many people have very different learning styles," Darren continued. "So, for instance, I might teach in a way that is how I would naturally learn, but I've never actually figured out their learning style."

Darren explained that when we don't know how people learn, it's more difficult to set clear expectations for them. He used an example of giving someone a list to follow. If that person's natural learning style is to process things verbally, they aren't likely to read the list. (I think I'm the list guy Darren was referring to in a not-so-subtle way. Let me riff and then we'll figure it out, OK?)

We all have different styles and preferences—for learning, for communication, for receiving appreciation. This is why as great leaders, we need to be all in for the individuals on our team, not just the whole team. We need to treat people *as they want to be treated.*

Over the years, a lot of entrepreneurs have expressed interest in seeing firsthand how we support our team, how we work together, what our work environment looks like, and how it functions. Every few months or so, I host a training and sharing session for business leaders, where I go over the research and the testing I'm immersed in at the time. As part of these events, we give a tour of our tiny office here in Boonton, New Jersey.

I find it fascinating that, in addition to asking our employees about the work environment, everyone seems to notice two things on the tour: the Dream Tree, which you learned about in chapter 8, and the Personal Operating Manuals (POMs). The POMs hang next to each person's workplace, next to a childhood school photo of them.

The idea for the manuals originated with Adrienne Dorison, my partner in Run Like Clockwork, the company that trains teams on the method I share in *Clockwork, Revised and Expanded.* Years ago, she shared a system she created to better empower communication between each team member. She called it the Employee Operating Manual.

Adrienne explained, "When you buy a new computer, or phone, or pretty much anything, it comes with an instruction manual that gives you an overview of how to use the product. Usually these manuals have a page in front that is like a cheat sheet, a summary of the most important instructions the buyer needs to make the thing run properly. You need a similar core instruction set for how to work with your colleagues."

I loved the idea immediately and designed it to best fit our company's needs. You could modify and rename this tool anything you like and fine-tune the elements you need, but the essence should stay the same. The POM is a one-page "cheat sheet" for how to communicate with, manage, and work with your team—and how they can work with each other, and with you. Since we implemented it at our office, it has eliminated friction, prevented miscommunications, and elevated camaraderie. The POMs allow you to instantly understand how a fellow teammate best communicates and where their natural strengths lie. The simple system truly works wonders.

Take a look at my POM and then I'll break it down for you:

PERSONAL OPERATING MANUAL FOR:	MIKE MICHALOWICZ
Style:	Maverick: Innovative, "outside the box" thinker, undaunted by failure.
Ability:	**Innate:** Autonomy, brainstorming, cheerleading, spokesperson, confidence **Potential:** Spots relevant patterns, future thinking and vision, confident in risk taking, seeks big impact, action oriented, simplifying the complex. **Experiential:** Public speaking, IT services, data forensic management, authorship, video recording, audio recording
Fragility:	Listening closely, details, analytics, adaptability, unfounded criticism
Appreciation:	Words of affirmation
Improvement:	Sandwich technique - what worked, what didn't and how to fix, and a positive push out of the gate. Give all the relevant facts of a situation.
Communication:	**Please Do:** Short bullet point directions. Brief sync up on personal/family and then let's get to work! Tell me what you know is fact and what you are guessing or assuming. **Please Don't:** Write me long emails, leave long messages, have long conversations. Tell me what you assume as if it was fact.
Personal / Professional Intentions:	**Personal:** Beach house, master guitar, maximized health, maximized personal finances, be the "destination location" for family/family gatherings. **Professional:** Leading business author, leading speaker, 25 business books.
Summary:	Mike is a verbal, animated, and stimulating communicator and projects enthusiasm and warmth. Strong sense of urgency and initiative and competitive drive to get things done. Understands people well and uses that understanding effectively in persuading others to willingly do what is required.

Figure 5.0

Here's how you create the POMs:

1. Employees fill out their own POMs. In this way, they have psychological ownership over them. If later they make significant changes, they discuss it with their boss to explain the changes.

2. Style: This is a one-sentence overview of the person's manner of behavior. We use the talent optimization tool called the Predictive Index. But there are many that I found to be excellent, including the ALL IN Assessment, StrengthsFinder, Myers-Briggs, Enneagram, and DISC.

3. Ability: Here we identify the person's experiential, innate, and potential abilities. Again, we use the behavioral and organizational tools to help with this. Also, each person is encouraged to adjust the document in a way that better suits how they see themselves.

4. Fragility: This is a list of the person's weaknesses, an area where there is low ability and no interest in seeking to develop it. This doesn't mean that everyone is free and clear of doing work related to their weaknesses, but we do our best to match people's strengths to the tasks that need them, and reduce/avoid having people do tasks that are in their zone of fragility.

5. Appreciation: This is based on Gary Chapman and Paul White's *The 5 Languages of Appreciation in the Workplace*. In their book they codify how we like to give and receive appreciation. They include words of affirmation, appropriate

physical touch, quality time, acts of service, and giving tangible gifts. When showing appreciation to a colleague, speak *their* language even if it is not naturally yours.

6. Improvement: This is how a person prefers to be corrected and supported. I might add that it should always be done in private.

7. Communication: These are the dos and don'ts that help a person feel comfortable communicating.

8. Personal/Professional Intentions: This is a short list of what we want to achieve personally and at work. When you understand each teammate's personal aspirations beyond work, you can support them, even if it is just acknowledging their goals.

9. Summary: This is an overview of the person and their personality. This is said in the employee's voice (meaning they write up the entire thing).

I have found the most impactful part of the POM is the Communication section, which helps us adapt to each other's unique styles and preferences without confusion or even discussion. We are all very different, and yet we all work well together. For example, Kelsey's says, "Tell me everything about your life. Bring your solutions, not just the problems and critiques." Whereas Erin's simply says, "Brevity." And I added the period, because you know, this is a book, and my editors made me. But on Erin's POM, she doesn't even have the period, because, you know, *brevity.*

Before we started using the POMs, I thought Kelsey was overly talkative. I thought she wasted time chatting. And I thought Erin was curt and sometimes rude. She gave one-word answers. She came off as standoffish. But the POM helped me understand them. Kelsey was being Kelsey and Erin was being Erin. Both are awesome colleagues. And now I know how each person prefers to communicate their awesomeness.

Beyond understanding and acceptance, the POM also gives me leverage. If I know in advance how Kelsey and Erin present, I can mirror it to the best of my ability. When I do that, they see that I care enough to communicate the way they do. Like traveling to a foreign country where you don't have the native tongue. If you just try a few words even with a gnarly accent, people care that you care enough to try.

Erin once told me, "I love it here. You guys get me." She feels that way because we more than accept her for who she is. We celebrate her for who she is. That empowers her to be herself *and* to feel a sense of belonging.

When you force people to comply, they seek to defy. When you embrace people as they are, they become rock stars.

The POMs also help us play into a person's strengths. When we first decided to implement one-on-ones, I assumed I should be the person doing it. I own the business, after all. But when you look at my POM, that doesn't make sense. My communication preference is a "brief sync up on personal/family and then let's get to work!" and I don't want to have "long conversations." How would that be helpful in a one-on-one? It wouldn't. The meetings would last about two minutes and we'd both leave frustrated, wondering why we bother with these meetings in the first place.

Looking at Kelsey's POM, it was a no-brainer—she should handle the one-on-ones. Kelsey's "tell me everything about your life" communication preference is one of the main reasons she's so great at one-on-ones. Our team values one-on-ones more than anything—over salary, vacation, health benefits, retirement plans, and recognition and rewards. To be clear, I am not suggesting they would forgo salary, benefits, and such for one-on-ones. What I am saying is that the one-on-ones bring such a significant benefit to them that they appreciate them more than all the other "bennies." They say the meetings are "like therapy with someone who is actively looking to support you and can act on that support." People *love* the time with Kelsey because Kelsey loves supporting them. Her support starts with deep listening, as noted on her POM.

Here's another example of the power of the POM. Erin is amazing at her job, and I wanted to thank her for a great project she completed. My natural tendency is to tell her, because *my* appreciation preference is "words of affirmation." Before I praised her, I looked at her POM. Her appreciation preference is "acts of service." Erin has a side hustle that replenishes cleaning supplies without the use of plastic containers. This is not a surprise—on her manual she noted that she loves nature. So to thank her, I signed up for her household supply service as a customer. This simple gesture meant more to her than any words. How could I tell? When I told her, she said, "I'm impressed!" For her, that's practically a monologue.

I have an annual tradition. The day before Christmas, I come into the office. No one is there, because we are closed from the week before the holiday through New Year's. I walk around the space in the silence, feeling grateful for all that we created. For the books we sell, for the work we get to do, for the people we serve. I also look at each and every coworker's Personal Operating Manual, grateful that each person has elected to include our company on their life's journey. In these moments, I'm reminded how our team works, communicates, appreciates, and thrives. It's a powerful way to resync with my team.

STRATEGY #3: LEAVE STATUS MANAGEMENT BEHIND

The traditional organizational chart is a pyramid. Typically the big cheese is at the very top, labeled something like "president." Or if that person drew the pyramid themselves, it might read: "Me." From the top, there's a long line down to the leaders, the Cs—CFO, CTO, CIO, COO. Then a line descends below each of them with more titles, and so on. This type of organizational chart is a "command and control" structure. Directions and instructions flow down from the top. Some of the better command-and-control organizations have feedback flow, where the folks on the bottom of the pyramid give leadership insights. No matter how you look at the pyramid, though, it's rigid, inflexible, massive, and weighty. And there's one really big problem: take out anyone in the chain of command and the communication flow breaks down. Take out the big cheese, and the system is completely in jeopardy.

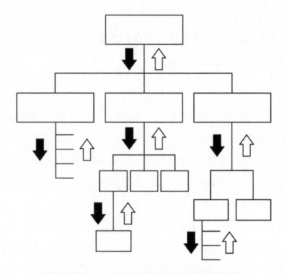

FIGURE 6.0 ■ **COMMAND and CONTROL**
In the traditional pyramid structure, commands are issued
from the top down, layer by layer, and feedback (assuming
bidirectional communication is encouraged) flows up layer
by layer. Communication can slow, and messages/intent
can dilute or change in the flow up and down.

A more effective organizational structure is a web. On a strength-to-density ratio, actual spiderwebs are stronger than steel. More important, spiderwebs are elastic. They can handle hurricanes and still remain intact, and they are better able to adjust to losses. Try this experiment yourself. Next time you see a web, pluck one strand. The single strand will break, by design, but the web structure will remain. The design of a web is such that if any individual strand breaks, the structure stays.

In business, strengthen direct communication flow between individuals. Leaders can give guidance, but individuals must be able to solve micro-problems on their own, to be nimble, and to have ownership over their roles.

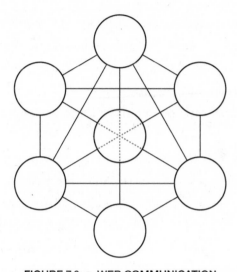

FIGURE 7.0 ▪ WEB COMMUNICATION
In the web structure, command and control flows to
individuals directly. The leader (center in this graphic)
is engaged in relevant communications to ensure a
maintained direction. Communication is faster, and
messages/intent are less likely to dilute or change.

At my first job out of college, I was part of a pyramid organizational chart, and I definitely experienced "command and control" from my Bad Boss. My Good Boss tried to bridge the pyramid to empower individuals, but my Bad Boss dominated and punished any efforts made outside the pyramid structure. Many talented employees left that company in part because of the organizational structure. Including, ultimately, Good Boss.

The command-and-control approach to leadership restricts innovation and malleability because it forces employees to manage status. I'll give you an example of a popular study. It involves a marshmallow challenge, but likely not the one you're thinking of. Peter Skillman, former VP of design at Palm and later at Nokia, introduced a simple team-building exercise to inspire creativity and innovation: the Marshmallow Design Challenge. Each group has eighteen minutes to construct a tower out of twenty sticks of spaghetti, one yard of tape, one yard of string, and one marshmallow. The goal is to build the tallest tower, with the marshmallow on top, without the structure toppling.

Teaming up with Tom Wujec, a fellow at Autodesk, the makers of AutoCAD design software, Skillman ran this exercise in design workshops with seventy groups, including Fortune 50 companies. In his TED Talk, "Build a Tower, Build a Team," Wujec explained that the worst results came from recent graduates of business school, and the best were recent graduates of kindergarten. "As Peter tells us [about the kindergartners]," Wujec said, "not only do they produce the tallest structures, but they are the most interesting structures of them all."

Why is this the case? Skillman and Wujec discovered that business grads spent a lot of time "jockeying for power" and trying to assess who was in charge—status management. They had learned command and control in school and tried to figure out their pyramid before they started playing with the spaghetti sticks. The kids didn't have that problem. They weren't worried about who was in charge, and they didn't think about a right way to do anything. They just worked together and tried stuff, and in the end, created better results.

It's time to leave the old-school command-and-control status management behind, don't you think?

HAPPIER PEOPLE ARE GOOD FOR BUSINESS

In 1971, the South Asian country of Bhutan was included in the United Nations' Least Developed Country (LDC) category, which tracks such metrics as gross national income and economic and environmental vulnerability. It's likely not a coincidence that one year later, the fourth king of Bhutan, Jigme Singye Wangchuck, declared, "Gross National Happiness is more important than Gross Domestic Product." According to the Oxford Poverty and Human Development Initiative, "The concept implies that sustainable development should take a holistic approach toward notions of progress and give equal importance to noneconomic aspects of well-being." In other words, they value happiness over how much wealth they can produce.

Bhutan then went on to create the Gross National Happiness Index (GNHI), which tracks standards in nine domains: psychological well-being, health, education, time use, cultural diversity and resilience, good governance, community vitality, ecological diversity and resilience, and living standards. And by the GNHI metrics, the people of Bhutan are considered the happiest in the world.

Have you ever been to Bhutan? I haven't yet. In fact, until I read the World Economic Forum's article about the country's sustainable development, I have to admit, I can't be certain I knew the country existed. You might think the rest of the article was about how the people "get by" without basic resources and don't seem to mind. Nosirree.

As I write this, Bhutan is next in line to "graduate" from the UN's LDC category. They have considerably improved their economic, environmental, and social situation over the past forty years. They have "recorded an average growth in annual GDP of 7.5 percent since the early 1980s and poverty levels have declined from 36 percent in 2007 to 10 percent in 2019." They have 100 percent electricity access for all people. And they have something none of us have: Bhutan is the only carbon-negative country in the world.

Happier people are good for business. When we invest in our employees' happiness and well-being, it will pay dividends in multiple areas. You've already gone a long way toward improving conditions for your team. If you look at the list of the Gross National Happiness Index's nine domains, you're making plans to cover quite a few of them. The goal is to continually work toward improving employee experience. It doesn't have to happen overnight. With intention and consistent action, it *will* happen, and your company will be stronger and more vital for it. What will be your Happiness Index for your team?

GOOD AND GREAT LEADERSHIP

Good Leaders	Great Leaders
Train for Job Growth Limiting an employee's growth ultimately limits their contribution to the company. Good leaders train their team to expand and improve their skill set so they can grow.	***Train for Job and Personal Growth*** Personal growth programs help your employees reach their potential and become the person they were meant to be. People value organizations that value them. Great leaders give their team opportunities for both job and personal growth.
Master Group Communication Inspired teams get things done—as long as they remain inspired. Good leaders develop strong motivational communication skills to empower their teams.	***Master Individual Communication*** People show and receive appreciation in different ways, and they have different skills and abilities, different strengths and weaknesses, and different communication styles. Great leaders don't treat everyone the same way. They treat people the way *they* want to be treated.
Prioritize Revenue Targets A business needs revenue to generate cash flow and it needs profit to be sustainable. Good leaders share and prioritize metrics with their team.	***Prioritize Happiness Targets*** You can't make people happy, but you can create an environment that fosters happiness and empowers them to seek it. Great leaders share revenue targets and *prioritize* happiness.

11

Adapt to Changing Work Environments

In 2003, two Best Buy employees, Calid Ressler and Jody Thompson, were developing new human resources guidelines when they saw an opportunity for a profound change. They proposed full autonomy for workers in exchange for full accountability. In other words, do what you agree to by the time you agreed to do it, but on a schedule that you want. Work from home anytime you want without needing to explain. No sick days, no vacation allotment, just get your commitments done.

And most radical, all meetings were now optional. You're invited by your manager, but if you don't think there is value for you to attend, then don't. The idea was managers would move to expecting the macro-outcomes: projects completed by such-and-such date, sales revenue increased by X percent during the quarter, and so forth. And they would drop the micro-measurements, such as a 9 a.m. start time and half-hour lunches. This is the Results-Only Work Environment, or ROWE.

Best Buy tested ROWE with office staff, not the people who worked at the retail stores. Makes sense. Imagine if everyone at your local Best Buy suddenly decided to skip coming in on Saturdays!

The experiment achieved four major wins: employees lives improved (e.g., most reported a gain of nearly one hour of additional sleep before starting workdays), voluntary turnover dropped by 90 percent on ROWE teams, and productivity went up 41 percent.

The fourth win: from 2003 to 2009, Best Buy had its best sustained growth ever.

In ROWE, leaders managed the company's output not by managing people but by empowering them. Thompson claimed, "When you get to take over your own life and feel responsible for yourself and your work, you feel proud and liberated and dignified." She added that the approach also shone a "bright light on people who'd previously been able to hide inside the system by showing up every day without accomplishing much."

Ressler and Thompson went on to write a book about ROWE, *Why Work Sucks and How to Fix It: The Results-Only Revolution*, and opened their own consulting firm to help other companies implement their approach.

Ten years later, new Best Buy CEO Hubert Joly canceled the company's ROWE commitment. He didn't want his team to "run free like unicorns," as Thompson had once stated. The company was in a downturn, and Joly wanted his team to return to in-person work. "Bottom line, it's 'all hands on deck' at Best Buy," he said. Which means, get your ass in the office!

Joly argued that ROWE was "fundamentally flawed from a

leadership standpoint." Effectively, he argued that the traditional command-and-control corporate model was replaced by nebulous, arbitrary delegation. The grand experiment was terminated not because it didn't work—remember, Best Buy had its best year-to-year growth and profitability ever during the grand ROWE experiment—but perhaps in part because bosses couldn't boss.

Despite Joly's return to in-person work, Best Buy's revenue had only marginal growth or decline, except for an outlier year of 2021, when everyone started spending like drunken sailors—*and* after Best Buy returned to a remote work environment for office-based teams due to Covid. Today, the company has adopted a hybrid approach. Employees are remote for deep work and together for collaborative work.

Regression to the old culture and policies, even if they are measurably less effective, is shockingly common. Best Buy had its best years during ROWE, yet they went back to the "traditional" work environment. Why? Because the comfort of doing what you have already done, even if it is less effective, or not at all effective, is easier than doing something different. Many leaders, it appears, can boldly stay only in their comfort zone.

Sometimes a new leader coming in just can't accept any variation on their standard policies and procedures. And sometimes a new work environment works well for a time, and then not so much. And sometimes you have both situations—rigidness and reality—in one leader.

When we change work environments to suit our own needs as leaders, or even in good faith for the good of the company, we must do so with deep consideration of how it will affect our employees' world. Otherwise, the change will not be well received. It shakes up the whole company ecosystem—leaders, employees, vendors, contractors, and customers. And when that change in environment tosses out FASO—when it disregards fit, ability, safety, and ownership—it can turn an all-in employee into a quiet quitter, or an actual quitter, in hours.

Changing a work environment takes time. People will be skeptical of it and you. You need to show your employees that you have considered them, that you are still all in on them, no matter what.

HUMANS NEED RELATIONSHIPS

Travis Ruskus is one of the world's leading rock balancers. You know what I am talking about—those stacked rock art structures that most people do in nature. The amateurs, cough . . . me . . . stack three flat rocks and post the "work of art" all over social media. Travis, though, stacks, balances, and arches rocks of all shapes and sizes. He creates structures that defy logic. And once they are complete, he films the collapse of the structure as he pulls out a keystone, returning the rock structure to where it belongs, randomly lying in the environment around it.

At a dinner with Travis one night, I asked him how he got into town. "By the UFO," he said as he cracked a lobster claw in his hand. After a moment of silence—because, well, how do you respond to that type of comment?—Travis looked up. "I call my van the UFO." Phew.

Turns out, Travis decked out a sprinter van that he now lives in year-round, minus the occasional replenishing and recuperating stay he does at his parents' house. He drives to whatever place interests him. He constantly meets new people. He sees every part of the world and has total freedom. And he loves that.

As we were finishing our meal, I asked him, "Any challenges on the road?"

"Yeah, it's lonely. It can get really f-ing lonely."

"But I thought you constantly meet new people."

"I do," he explained. "It isn't about meeting new people. The problem is I don't see the same people."

Ah, yes, to stave off loneliness, we need the *same* people. We need our community, that constant. We need the comfort of communal familiarity, which provides us a sense of significance in this world. A sense of belonging.

Humans need relationships with humans. Long-term, in-person relationships.

And a company that fosters those types of relationships becomes the center of their lives.

In his article for the *Harvard Business Review*, "Work and the Loneliness Epidemic," former US surgeon general Vivek Murthy argues that despite our increasing connectedness through technology, society is seeing rising levels of loneliness—and this was prepandemic. And it's not just our employees who feel this. More than 50 percent of CEOs feel lonely in their job.

Murthy states, "This isn't just bad for our health; it's also bad for business. Researchers for Gallup found that having strong social connections at work makes employees more likely to be engaged with their jobs and produce higher-quality work, and less likely to fall sick or be injured. With strong social connections, these gains become losses."

How do we combat loneliness at work? Murthy calls on companies to "make fostering social connections a strategic priority." But how do we do that when work environments are in a seemingly constant state of change? When many employees expect to work from home? When so many companies have teams all over the country, or the globe?

At my company, the solution has been face-to-face time. For those who live locally, we meet multiple times a week. We keep our small office for those who want to work in-person. The office is full on Tuesdays and Thursdays when we have more involved huddles. We make sure to have a meal together. For those who live outside New Jersey (why would anyone choose to live anywhere but the Garden State?), we fly them in for an in-person, full-day meeting every quarter and an annual multiday retreat.

As a result, our team is connected and strong. We know each other as real people, not moving video images. My colleagues tell me, "I love coming to the office" and "I love my wamily" (work family).

We can combat loneliness at work by ensuring that everyone on the team meets face-to-face at least every quarter, or ideally more often. And that the primary goal of those meetings is facilitating in-person human connection.

FIND YOUR BLEND

People say they are more productive from home. And that is likely true—for a little while. At a certain point, when all we do is work from home, we aren't really more productive. Life settles in. We work in short bursts and jump around from personal to business.

When we were at work, we would work then drift off or go down a social media rabbit hole, or bullshit with a colleague, killing two people's time with one stone.

Maybe from home we are "more productive" in some ways, but we are less productive in others. Without others we lose the productivity of brainstorming, impromptu moments, differing perspectives, and collaboration. We lose connection.

In a conversation with a *Bloomberg* journalist, Stanford economist

Nick Bloom shared a story about working with James Liang, co-founding CEO and chairman of one of the world's largest travel agents, Trip.com. The first was in 2011. Liang wanted to evaluate work-from-home because they had a large call center in Shanghai, where the office space cost a pretty penny. The result of their 250-person randomized controlled trial was they discovered that productivity went up 13 percent for employees working from home.

In 2021, Bloom and Liang conducted their second experiment, this time focused on hybrid work. *Bloomberg* states, "They took 1,600 people that are coders, finance and marketing professionals—around 25 percent managers, and randomized between fully in the office and working from home two days a week." The results showed that while performance remained about the same or slightly better, "the big benefit was that quit rates dropped by a third and employees' job satisfaction, work-life balance and intention to stay in the firm were significantly higher."

Personally, my most successful approach is to bifurcate tasks. For example, when it comes to writing, I work best on airplanes. Writing at work is hard unless I lock myself in the office and wear earplugs. But when it comes to planes, I can write for eight hours straight. I don't want to have eye contact with strangers, nor they with me. I don't get the WiFi, so no distractions. I just write.

I also write at home, from 5:30 a.m. to around 7 a.m. every weekday, and I do that over a video conference with a handful of fellow authors working away on their books. (Connection matters!)

Banging out emails seems well suited for the home office. But when it comes to doing videos, my office at the office is best. And of course, for brainstorming new products and idea generation for my books (including this one), my office at the office is most definitely the best, with the team there. In fact, every other Tuesday is a brain-storm and strategy day and usually a group lunch.

True optimal output comes about with planned variability. Consider it like cross-training for athletics—mix things up to optimize your performance for your best thing. In your one-on-ones with employees, figure out what is optimal for them and build a structure around them that factors in different approaches based on their tasks. Find what works for them and what brings everyone together. In other words, find the blend.

PRESENTEEISM

In the fifth grade, I received a "perfect attendance" award. It was given to the students who didn't miss a single day of school. I didn't have the best grades, but I did know that if I just showed up, I would get kudos. So that became my thing: never miss a day of school. Which later became never miss a day of work. And for over a decade, I would go in no matter what. Sick as a dog, I am still going in. Could I get others sick? Sure, but they could work through it too. Other times I missed family events and my kids' school activities. But those were the sacrifices they, I mean I, needed to make.

Presenteeism is a phenomenon that results in declined (or no) productivity when a team member is not able to fully function because of illness, injury, exhaustion, emotional distraction, compromised relationships, or other causes. People are at work, but out of it. This is different than goofing off or inability. This is when a person's average work level drops because they can't physically or emotionally be fully present or capable.

Emerging evidence, as reported in the *Harvard Business Review*, indicates that simple screening, treatment, and education can amplify productivity. The good news: you're already all in on the one-on-ones, which automatically have this screen built in. When you have a weekly dialogue about your employee's emotional and physical state, it's harder for them to hide it. When they are encouraged to take care of themselves and understand that their health and well-being are integral to the company's success, they are also less likely to *fight* through it.

The challenge is, we laud presenteeism. Did you hear the story about Kevin Ford, the airport Burger King employee who never missed a day of work in twenty-seven years? His story was all over the news because in recognition for his perfect attendance, Ford received—drum roll, please—a goodie bag with some Reese's Pieces, a Starbucks drink cup, and a coupon for a free movie ticket. Wah-wah.

I understand why the news outlets framed the story about his peculiar gift, but I think the real story was about the cost of his perfect attendance. He must have come in sick to work a few times over the years. He likely missed more than a few important family events. And in twenty-seven years, surely people he loved needed him from time to time, and he couldn't help them, because he was dutifully handing out Whoppers and fries.

I also understand that some people *cannot* miss a day of work, because they need every penny they can earn. This is where Ford's leaders failed him. Not just because their recognition for his service was a dud—a dud he loved, by the way, because he's a gracious gem of a human—but because they totally missed his sacrifices and the toll it took on him. In a video interview, Ford said, "I would love to have a day off to visit friends, have some fun and relax . . . I can't even think about a day off, I haven't had a day off in so long." Twenty-seven years, to be exact.

I guess that movie ticket will have to wait—forever.

As you adapt to changing work environments, remember that showing up just to show up is not productive for your team or your company. And the cost is everything missed.

QUIET QUITTING

Every employee who leaves a company always leaves their employer twice. First in their heart, and then in their body.

I didn't realize it, but I am a "quiet quitter." Or at least was. Quiet quitting is when an employee checks out, stops caring, and, in some cases, stops working entirely, but remains on staff. They do all this quietly, expecting that no one will notice. And most leaders don't.

When I had my one and only corporate job, I sucked at it. Not because I wanted to, at least not in the beginning. Remember my story about selling our forensics company to Robert Half International? We were ignored for weeks and then placed into roles that made zero sense. The part of that story I didn't tell was about a conversation I had when I finally went into the corporate office in Manhattan. The building was on Avenue of the Americas a few blocks from Rockefeller Center, where they proudly display the big Christmas tree every year.

When I arrived, Tina, the HR person, walked me to a small desk. "You'll work here," she said. Then she gave me my objectives. "You need to be billable at least thirty-six hours a week. Arrive by eight a.m. Attend weekly telephone conferences. John, your boss, likes to stay late. So make sure you're available to answer questions. Good luck."

Before she turned to walk away, I said, "Question for you. I would like to sit over there, with the other folks who I will be working mostly with. Can I move my desk?"

Tina laughed. "Sorry, Mike. You are not at that level yet." Then she walked away.

As I stated earlier, when we are forced to comply, we will seek a way to defy.

In that moment, my heart left. It was so clear to me that I was filling in a blank. No one cared about me. They just cared about the output from me.

With my heart gone my quiet quitting began. What if I didn't produce the thirty-six billable hours? What if I didn't wait around until John left for the night? What if I didn't even come to the office? I found another Robert Half location in New Jersey that was half the commute. I would go there to fill in my required time at the office.

I didn't bill thirty-six hours, and they didn't care right away. At my six-month review, they told me I didn't produce enough and cut my salary. This "punishment" was not really an incentive to work harder. In fact, it incentivized me to resent them more. Reciprocity works both ways. A kind deed engenders a kind deed. Disregard begets disregard.

You know the rest of the story. When the boss came to me and said, "My God, we need you to lead this," there was no way I would agree. I couldn't care less about a company that couldn't care less about me. I was just buying time until the inevitable termination. I wasn't harming the company or doing anything against it. But surely, I didn't do anything to grow it.

My body left eleven months and one week after I was hired. My heart left on the first day.

Quiet quitting is less about the employee and more about the employer. Yes, people exist to milk the system. The professional "slip and fall" folks. The people who get a job and then don't show up and then file for unemployment. The people who naturally do the bare minimum. But they are the exception. Here are two truths I know from experience:

1. The majority of people want to work to the best of their ability and thrive when supported in doing just that.

2. The majority of people want to live their best life and thrive when supported in doing just that.

Sadly, employers occasionally miss on the first one, and almost always on the second one.

Quiet quitting happens when an employee realizes that regardless of their effort it will never be enough. It will never move them to where they want to be. And they conclude that the employer is trying to wring out as much as possible from them before they give up and quit. Employees are simply giving up on caring and developing a strategy to bring balance to themselves. To care for themselves.

So they check off the lowest standard. They do just enough to not justify a causal termination. The employer becomes a rental car agency: return the car with a full tank, no scratches or dents, and a clean interior. So what do we do? We do donuts in the parking lot. Peel out at lights. And never ever fill the gas tank.

Quiet quitting is a result of ignoring FASO. The leader skips safety and ownership. It can be a leader who doesn't care enough to be great. Or it is a new leader deploying comfortable, old leadership approaches.

YOU DON'T HAVE EMPLOYEES

"They *used* to be called employees, Boomer." My twentysomething daughter said this to me when I showed her some excerpts from this book during the early stages of writing it. I wanted to correct her immediately—I'm Gen X, the acid-washed jean generation. Not. A. Boomer. But it is comforting to learn and be shunned at the same time.

I had proudly showed Adayla my newest ideas and research, and she stopped after reading the first line: "Great leaders make their employees believe not in them, but in themselves." Admittedly it was a clunky line. But I like to think it had a John F. Kennedy–ish ring to it. "Ask not . . ." and all that.

After she shot down my rising phoenix of a book, she explained what she meant. The term "employee" has a narrow definition— someone who works for a specific company, to achieve specific outcomes, within specific time frames. Today, a company is composed of a mix of individuals. Vendors, subcontractors, virtual help, full-time, part-time, per diem employees, term employees, volunteers, interns, and so on.

We don't have employees. We have a team. A group of specialists who have come together for a period of time to accomplish a goal. Everyone plays a role, is given objectives, and coordinates their effort to achieve a shared vision. Just like a sports team has players who utilize their specific abilities in their roles to achieve their objectives and the collective's objectives (like win the division championship, for example).

"Team" is the word now, and this Gen X-er is going to use it.

GOOD AND GREAT LEADERSHIP

Good Leaders	Great Leaders
Mandate Remote/In-Person Work Policies An in-person attendance policy isn't bad. It speaks to a standard. But think of what serves your team the best. What allows them to be the best of themselves. In some cases, you absolutely need people's physical presence (e.g., retail, medical services, transportation). Good leaders make policies that best serve the company and the employees.	**Allow Employees to Find Their Remote/In-Person Blend** Some employees work better in a physical office. Others are happier and more productive working remotely. And some prefer a combination of the two. Great leaders encourage their team to experiment and discover where they work best.
Reward Effort Rewarding employees for a job well done demonstrates that you value their contributions. Celebrating best attempts is important, as it helps them develop their potential. Good leaders reward effort, not just outcomes.	**Reward Recovery** Team burnout is not only dangerous for them; it's dangerous for your company. Exhausted teams are not high performers, and they cannot reach their potential. Taking time off allows employees to recharge their batteries, which then makes it easier for them to contribute fresh ideas. Great leaders reward taking time for recovery.

12

Let People Go

An employee tried to flatten our president."

When I heard this, I did a spit take. I've heard some employee rage stories, but this one may be the rage-iest. In an interview with small-business attorney Nancy Greene, author of *Navigating Legal Landmines*, I asked her if she had any "juicy" stories about employee dismissals gone bad. That's when she told me this whopper.

"A Black construction worker thought he was exempt from being fired because he was in a protected class," Nancy started. She went on to explain that he had a long list of documented performance issues, including unexplained absences, showing up late for work, and walking off the job site to take personal calls. He had been warned he might be fired, but he kept up his unsatisfactory performance, and filed a discrimination claim with the US Equal Employment Opportunity Commission (EEOC). The EEOC is an important safe harbor for marginalized employees who are being discriminated against by their employers. It was an odd choice for this guy, though, because his boss was *also* Black.

When the employee was told he would still be fired if he didn't make the required improvements, he became furious and stormed out of the office. "Later that day," Nancy said, "our president, who was this tiny, sweet, seventy-year-old African American man, left the office to go home. Before he could get into his car, a pickup came out of nowhere and tried to run him over. It was the furious, about-to-be-fired employee. "Fortunately, our president was a *spry* seventy-year-old. He dodged out of the way and slid between two cars. Thankfully, he wasn't hit."

The next day, the employee was fired. He then filed another discrimination complaint. It was Nancy's job to file the response. "I submitted affidavits to the EOCC saying, 'Here's the ten people who saw him try to hit the company president with his truck.'" Unsurprisingly, the EOCC did not pursue his claim.

Wild, right? This story is an extreme example of what can happen when an employee does not expect to be fired. Sure, the murderous construction worker had been told he would be fired, but he thought it couldn't happen because of the complaint he filed. When he realized he would be fired anyway, he lost it. Or as they sometimes say in the South, he "dropped his basket."

As CEO of N D Greene PC, a law firm based in northern Virginia that specializes in small-business employment law, Nancy has helped hundreds of companies navigate the complicated—and often emotional—world of hiring and firing. In our conversation, she shared solid advice for progressive discipline, termination, and compliance with employment law. I'll give you the best stuff I learned from her in this chapter. But in consideration of everything there is to share, the most important takeaway is this:

Someone losing their job should never be surprised by it.

If you adhere to that intent, the actions you take will naturally be the best-suited actions. Most people aren't going to react the way the murderous construction guy did, but that doesn't mean they won't be upset. And when we care so much about our team, that's the last thing we want. In fact, I'd go so far as to say we don't want to let anyone go—especially after working the FASO method and investing in a person's potential.

If only dismissing someone was simple. You identify a team member who is underperforming for the roles they need to fulfill, and they would not be a good fit for any other role in the company. You ask them to improve and give them direction on how to do it. They try, but they're still not cutting it. You say, "I'm sorry, you didn't improve." They say, "Thank you for the report," and then walk out the door without an issue, maybe waving goodbye with a Vulcan hand sign meaning "Live long and prosper." The sad reality is, when most people leave, there's a hand gesture for sure—just not the Vulcan one.

Here I come with my Chief Disruptor hat on, to challenge your assumptions with this question: does firing *have* to be a negative? What if when we make the difficult decision to let someone go, it turns out to be a good thing—for everyone, including the person who is being let go? I can't promise this will always be the case. Some people are asshats, plain and simple. Some people get bored and draw eyes on million-dollar paintings. Some people lie about their grandmother dying so they can take time off to party in the Bahamas. And some people try to run over their boss with their pickup truck.

For those non-jerks, the people who, despite all their efforts—and yours—just aren't the right fit for your company, being let go doesn't have to be a sad or a messy ending. It could be the beginning of something great.

Think about pro athletes. Some leave the business of on-the-field competition and go on to be sportscasters. Other athletes stick around after they peak and fade to oblivion. The fit is no longer there but they keep un-retiring to compete "just one more year." Others are encouraged to walk and take that as an opportunity to express unexplored potential.

Former Steelers quarterback Terry Bradshaw has expounded away for decades as a sportscaster. Tennis great and line-judge antagonist John McEnroe continues to be the king of pontificating on television. And Tara Lipinski, a 1998 Olympic gold medalist figure skater, won't try to qualify for the next Olympics. She is an alumna of the skating profession and now a famous commentator for the skating profession. When the current fit is no longer there, you can empower people to find their next fit. Their next chapter.

Letting people go is healthy for the organization and, almost always, for the person you are letting go. Many leaders hold on to people, thinking they are serving that person when in fact they are hurting them—and the company. And they use the justification to avoid a hard (albeit honest) conversation.

The reality is, the longer you keep someone on staff who is not a fit, the longer you are keeping them from a job opportunity that *is* a fit. The longer you're keeping them from the experiences, community, and recognition they deserve. A great leader doesn't need to protect an employee from hurt feelings or hold them back from something great. Yes, letting someone go triggers emotions and loss, but at the same time, it opens the door for the future. If potential can't be expressed with you, don't you have a responsibility to allow that person to express their potential elsewhere?

HIRE SLOW, FIRE SLOWER

A popular employment dictum is "Hire slow. Fire fast." But what if that approach is wrong? Or at least misunderstood? Maybe we should say, "Hire slow. Fire slower."

Hiring slow makes good sense. When we hire methodically, matching fit to ability, and take the time to assess a candidate's potential, the need to fire will happen less frequently. When we don't take the time to ensure we've clearly detailed the Primary Job and other responsibilities for a position, the new employee starts the job at a disadvantage. And when we hire based on résumés and interviews alone, and don't take the time to assess a candidate's ability and potential, and ensure a complement to the company's environment, we could be setting that employee up for failure right from the get.

Firing fast, on the other hand, may not be the best approach. The idea is, once you know for sure a person is not a good fit for your company, don't hesitate to let them go. That part also makes sense, but we tend to leap to that conclusion without doing our due diligence. It's as if we flip a switch—an employee is good until they're not.

Remember, great leaders are all in for their employees, and that includes taking the time to figure out *why* someone isn't working out and if there's anything you can do about it. That's the "fire slower" part—don't start the firing process until you're sure it's the best course of action. If you were slow and deliberate in hiring someone, and then they don't work out as planned, there may be an opportunity for a course correction (unless the issue is egregious).

When an employee is underperforming, take these steps before you start the firing process:

1. Try to first correct the employee's behavior. Often something that should have been communicated, or you think was communicated, wasn't. Tell them what you are observing and what your thoughts are on how to improve or fix it.

2. If the behavior does not improve, consider if there could be a different path for them in your organization. This is a process I call "re-fitting."

3. Re-interview the employee to get a sense of their interest. What do they want to do? Have they discovered anything while on the job that shifted their goals or desires?

4. Re-measure the employee for fit. Did you miss something? Would they be better in a different role?

5. If there is colleague conflict—for example, this team member brings a dark cloud with them and everyone's performance is affected—explain the impact they are having on others. Ask them what actions they can take to make everyone, including them, have more joy working together.

If you've exhausted every option to find the right place for an employee you once thought would be great for your company, it's time to let them go. We'll get to how to do that in a moment. First, let's go over how to have those first difficult conversations with your employee about not measuring up.

HOW TO HAVE DIFFICULT CONVERSATIONS

If you follow the Retention Rhythm detailed in chapter 7, you'll have the single most powerful tool to get in front of performance issues: the weekly one-on-ones. When you know what's up with an employee—their work projects, their personal and professional goals, concerns they have about their work community, their interests, and any personal challenges they may be having—it's much easier to deal with issues as they come up. When you notice an employee is struggling in some way or not meeting expectations, you can address it in a nonthreatening way and work together to come up with a solution.

For example, Terry (not Terry Bradshaw) is new to our team. She is a great employee. She's driven and eager to learn. As I mentioned earlier, we have an annual three-day company retreat. Terry scheduled a trip to Italy that conflicted with the retreat. She didn't ask if she could miss the retreat, she just booked the trip. In her one-on-ones with Kelsey, Terry mentioned her dream to travel to Italy, and that she had booked the trip. When Kelsey asked her about her dates, they were in direct conflict with the retreat.

In their conversation, Kelsey learned that Terry didn't realize the company retreat was a mandatory meeting. We need all employees at the meeting because that's when we brainstorm together and plan the year ahead. Kelsey explained that Terry was expected to attend the retreat, and Terry adjusted her flights as best she could to at least be there for the core part of the retreat. If we didn't have the weekly one-on-ones, Kelsey might not have discovered this issue in time for Terry to correct it.

Terry didn't intentionally schedule a conflict; it was just an oversight. And I may be partly (mostly) to blame. Due to a keynote invite that came in at the last minute, I asked to move our retreat dates only a few months in advance, when normally it is planned a year out. Many mistakes, oversights, and miscues are unintentional and due to a communication breakdown. Fixing them with care and candor usually fixes them forevermore. I may be wrong, but I strongly suspect Terry won't schedule to be away again during a retreat.

Our job as leaders is not to call employees out for underperforming or making a mistake. Our job is to figure out *why* they are underperforming or made a mistake and determine what conditions would foster optimal performance. In other words, we can't just ask our employees to fix their behavior; we have to do our part and make any necessary fixes to their work environment.

All one-on-one meetings with employees, whether weekly check-ins or formal disciplinary meetings, should be done in private. In the meeting, avoid using phrasing that amounts to saying, "I'm right and you're wrong." Instead, use language that shows you are curious and you are listening, such as, "Here's what I've observed. What are your thoughts?"

An effective way to have difficult conversations with employees is to leverage Gestalt principles.

Gestalt is a type of psychology started in Germany by Max Wertheimer. The word "Gestalt" means "shape" or "form." The idea is to look at the totality of the mind, the complete whole, rather than the parts. So rather than look at each mistake an employee made, each issue they may be having, look at the whole picture.

Part of Gestalt principles is Gestalt Language Protocol. It was designed to manage a relationship through difficult conversations. This strategy helps you avoid getting into a debate with a teammate, where one person is defending and the other is attacking, and so forth. Here are the guidelines to follow:

1. Don't give direct advice. Speak from your own experience.

2. Don't give embedded advice. For example, avoid saying, "Have you considered . . . ?" or "Did you try . . . ?"

3. Use "I" statements rather than "you" statements.

4. Share the specifics and share both the positive and negative about it.

5. Share why you are asking what you are asking before you ask. This is not a trial.

6. Instead of asking "Why?," ask "How?" Don't ask, "Why did you do that?" Instead ask, "How did you get to that decision?"

7. To get clarity, paraphrase: "What I hear you saying . . ."

THE SANDWICH TECHNIQUE

The Sandwich Technique is a mindful way of addressing difficult topics with colleagues. I love this critical feedback technique because it is easy to remember. I mean, who doesn't love a good sammy? The process is also simple to execute and highly effective. In short, it is a piece of good news (a slice of bread), which opens the person to listening. The next part is addressing the problem to fix (the meat, or portobello mushroom for my vegetarian friends). And the last part is another piece of good news, which could be encouragement or supportive evidence of their historical progress (the other slice of bread).

Let's say an employee consistently shows up late for company meetings. Here's how you could employ the Sandwich Technique to address that issue:

Bread (good news): "I appreciate how enthusiastic you are in our brainstorming sessions. You bring such powerful out-of-the box thinking. And we used that specific idea you had last week. Thanks for that."

Meat (problem to fix): "I noticed that recently you have been arriving late for our online meeting. Do you know what I am talking about?" Wait for confirmation, and perhaps explanation. Then add, "We delay the meeting at times for you, and other times when you come late everyone greets you and it disrupts our momentum. Can you arrive a few minutes early for each meeting?" Discuss the options and suggest alternatives. For example, if they arrive late to an online meeting, they might keep their camera off and their microphone muted. If the meeting is in-person, and they have a conflict that will cause them to be late, they might agree to skip the meeting or ask if it could be pushed back to accommodate them.

Bread (more good news): "We are all looking to improve the business. I appreciate how open you are to honest feedback and your willingness to tweak your own schedule and support the company. I'm excited to hear your ideas at our next brainstorm on Tuesday."

Do you see how the Sandwich Technique is one of empowering, rather than shaming? During the "Meat" part of the process, remember to first see if there is shared clarity on the problem. Then ask them for their thoughts about how to move forward. Let the employee create the solution. This gives them—you guessed it—psychological ownership. (I will beat that drum until the end of time.)

When you use this technique, don't try to address everything at once, because it could feel overwhelming to that person. Instead, prioritize the most pressing issue, the big thing. Fix that first. Once it's improved, Sandwich the next challenge.

HOW TO KNOW WHO TO LET GO

You've addressed fit, had the difficult conversations, and you think it may be time to initiate the firing process. How can you be sure this is the right decision? The main reason to let someone go is if by keeping this person it would be detrimental to the firm. They are either not contributing to the firm or not contributing as well as expected, or their presence at the firm hurts the company in another way. Grounds for firing might include:

- Performance (they don't meet expectations, miss work)

- Cost (your company can't afford them, downsizing)

- Disruption (the person is compromising the performance of others)

- Reputation (the person is damaging the reputation of the organization)

- Criminal (the person is conducting criminal activity, e.g., theft within or outside the company)

- Harassment (bullying, sexual harassment)

- Lying (lies on application, on work performance, reporting work, unethical behavior, etc.)

■ Drugs/alcohol (illegal use, unable to perform, etc.)

■ Community mismatch (they are disharmonious with the community you are building)

■ Policy violations (they violate the rules of the company)

The list above is pretty standard stuff. When deciding if it's time to start the firing process, we can also learn from the reasons why we might let go of a personal relationship. In an article for Mindbody green.com, Sarah Regan shares advice from marriage and family therapist Shelly Bullard, who offers fourteen signs it's time to let go. I've adapted the list for business:

1. You don't feel comfortable or safe around them, emotionally or physically. You don't feel you can trust them. That Spidey sense is there for a reason. And when it comes to personal safety, our gut must be trusted.

2. You (or someone else on your team) is doing the work for them. When one team member suddenly seems to be working more hours, they may be taking on someone else's work.

3. They have a draining effect on everyone in the office. People feel they need to dance around this person or treat them with kid gloves.

4. The business has outgrown them. The first people on board will rarely be the last people on board. Things change, and sometimes a person is no longer a fit. Or sometimes they have

outgrown the business. They want more—more benefits, more responsibility, more opportunities for growth—and your company doesn't have more to give.

5. Their performance is dropping continuously, and despite having those difficult conversations, they have not improved.

6. Your employees don't want to work with them.

7. They are insubordinate.

8. You keep thinking you should let them go.

That last one is just as important as the rest, because we can't ignore the nagging feeling that something isn't right. Great leaders know when they know, you know?

HAVE YOU UNDERPERFORMED?

Before you fire someone for underperforming, conduct an honest review of how you and your company may have underperformed for this individual.

Did you provide them with the physical, psychological, and financial safety they needed to do their best work? Did you give them psychological ownership over some aspect of their role? Were you invested in their goals and dreams? Were you committed to building and fostering community, and ensuring they felt they belonged? Did you follow the Retention Rhythm? Have you given them opportunities to grow and up-level their performance?

Here are a few other questions to consider:

1. Have you engaged them in regular dialogue? One-on-ones?

2. Have you explored ways to support their goals and dreams through their work? Even if it is just regularly checking in on their goals and dreams?

3. Have you expressed gratitude to your team?

4. Have you gone the extra mile for your team?

5. Have you helped your colleague find and develop their potential?

THE FINAL FIFTEEN MINUTES

When Nancy Greene shared that sweet, sweet wisdom, "Someone losing their job should never be surprised by it," I asked her to share the protocol she recommends.

She explained, "You're not legally required to do progressive discipline, but you've invested time and energy in that person. The goal as the employer is never to lose an employee with potential. You want them to be there ten years, fifteen years, twenty years."

Progressive discipline is basically a series of imperative conversations in which you address the issues at hand, work together to solve them, and, should the issues persist, address the consequences—including potentially getting fired. Nancy recommends documenting every conversation in writing to back up verbal communication.

If you know you may be headed toward firing someone, learn the law in advance. When you are ready to fire, you want to be sure you are in compliance and have legal standing to do so. Remember, labor laws vary state by state (and country by country), so if your employee is a remote worker living in a different locality than the one your business is located in, you'll need to make sure you are in compliance with that location's laws.

Nancy explained that many legal issues and friction can be prevented by ensuring company policies are in writing, which eliminates misunderstandings. It is important that employees understand what rights they have to physical property, such as laptops; to intellectual property; client lists; and other proprietary information. Noncompete clauses and nondisclosure agreements must also be in place before you fire someone. This will make the final step as smooth as possible for everyone.

When you've been through the entire "fire slower" process and you're ready to let someone go, that final meeting should not be more than fifteen minutes long. Nancy explained that it's never a long meeting because it's not a fight. "The decision's been made. You are just informing them and giving them their final paperwork, but they know it's coming. And if they really haven't seen it coming at this point, it's because you haven't given them the heads-up."

When I asked Nancy how to have this ultimate difficult conversation, she said, "Tell them, 'Hey, we've had these discussions. You've understood. You've heard my concerns with your performance. I'm sure you've felt frustrated in the position. It's time for the company and you to move on.' Because you've had all those leading-up discussions, this final meeting is not a surprise."

MAINTAIN YOUR COMMITMENT TO SEEING POTENTIAL IN EVERYONE

As I mentioned at the start of this chapter, it is the ultimate unselfish move to empower an employee to fulfill their potential elsewhere—particularly if there is no opportunity to fulfill that potential at your company. A push out the door may be just what they need to become who they want.

Lisa Palazzi worked for me as a personal assistant for about a year. Try as she might, she just wasn't the right fit for that role. She did her best to manage my schedule, but it was just not her thing. On the first day of onboarding, where the team share trivia about themselves, we discovered that Lisa has a passion for firefighting. She had massive potential in that area, but we didn't have an opportunity for her to grow into that. I mean, unless someone started burning my books—which some of the reviews I get indicate would be a better choice than reading them. But even then, it would be a bucket-of-water type of situation, surely not a fire engine.

What we *did* have, though, was the ability to let her have the flexibility to explore her interest. Because everyone saw that she would be great as a firefighter and supported it, she reciprocated by doing the best she could with my schedule, even though it wasn't her passion. She kept us going while we looked for someone who would be a better fit, and we kept her going while she looked for opportunities to reach her potential—outside of the company. And here is the surprising part. Lisa did a better job as a scheduler than most people who tried to fill that role for me. Why? The power of reciprocity. Care for the person's true interests, and they will care for yours.

Twelve months later, Lisa found her dream job as an airport firefighter in Georgia, and we found the perfect person to handle my schedule, Erin. We saw Lisa's potential when we hired her, and we didn't stop seeing it just because she was the wrong fit for the job we needed her to do.

Letting Lisa go was not a messy, negative experience. It was a joyful experience because we both won. The real proof of this is, six months after she left our company, Lisa asked if she could come to our annual company retreat to participate with the team. She didn't have to do that; she *chose* to do that. And she did this on her own dime and her own time because she wanted to give us her ideas to help grow the business. Plus, we learned not to start the house's fireplace without opening the flue. Fire averted.

Again, I ask you, does firing have to be negative? What if when we make the difficult decision to let someone go, it turns out to be a good thing—for everyone, including the person who was fired? We should reframe "letting someone go" to "letting someone flourish." Imagine a plant you put in the shade. It struggles to grow. You try to water it, fertilize it, sing show tunes to it, but no matter what you do, it continues to wither. If you transfer it to a new location where it can get the sun it needs to grow, the plant will thrive.

You don't have to frame a dismissal as a dismissal; it can be a transition to alumni status. At our office we have an alumni wall, with Lisa, Liz, Jake, and Maritza. All former active colleagues who have moved on to explore their potential elsewhere. All still admired by our company. All still offering support and insight and showing up when we, or they, ask.

THE "BETTER NEXT TIME" SELF-EVALUATION

When there is a mismatch between fit and ability with an employee, it is an opportunity to investigate what might have gone wrong. Failure is a key part of learning. Maybe you hired someone for one position and ended up giving them completely different jobs to do. You may need to adjust the must-haves lists for the next person. Maybe a person's demonstrated interest in workshops waned over time, a sign of a cap on that specific potential. You may need to find a new exercise for the event that reveals a person's interest beyond curiosity.

In her TED Talk, "Increase Your Self-Awareness with One Simple Fix," organizational psychologist Tasha Eurich states that most people (95 percent) think they are self-aware, but only a small fraction (less than 15 percent) of us are. That's a big gap! We think we know ourselves, but few of us do.

In her book *Insight: The Surprising Truth About How Others See Us, How We See Ourselves, and Why the Answers Matter More Than We Think*, Eurich reveals results from three years of research on self-awareness. That research showed what truly self-aware people, the 15 percent, do differently. And it has to do with the type of questions they ask themselves.

Eurich says to start to become more self-aware, "We just need to change one simple word. Change 'why' to 'what.' Why-questions trap us in that rearview mirror. What-questions move us forward to our future."

A great leader reflects on their part in things. Rather than blame a firing on the employee who didn't work out, or someone else, or circumstances, take the time to evaluate yourself and your company. This is not a "why did it go wrong?" shame-fest. This is you asking, "What can I do better to ensure the next person is an ideal fit?" and then taking action on what you've learned.

I've created the "Better Next Time" self-evaluation tool, which you can download at Theallincompany.com/start. I recommend you fill out the entire form and take steps to make improvements. For now, here are a few "what" questions to consider as you gain self-awareness about your leadership:

1. What changes do I need to make to this position's must-haves (responsibilities, qualities, and qualifications) to ensure the next person is a better fit?

2. What more can I do to identify abilities and potential in candidates?

3. What can I do to enhance physical, psychological, and financial safety for my team?

4. What more can I do to foster psychological ownership in employees?

5. What more can I do to nurture potential in employees?

6. What more can I do to help employees be more of who they are at work?

GOOD AND GREAT LEADERSHIP

Good Leaders	Great Leaders
Terminate Employees If an employee's performance is inadequate or their potential cannot be filled at the company, they will need to move on. Good leaders make sure employee terminations are not a surprise.	**Graduate Employees** When an employee's existing ability and potential ability is outside of the roles/needs the business has, they should be directed to fulfill their potential elsewhere. Their history will always be part of the business. And in some cases, an affinity can be maintained. Great leaders do everything in their power to pave the path forward for terminated employees.
Hire Slow, Fire Fast Hiring quickly to fill an urgent need results in bad hires. When someone is truly not a fit, they need to move on from the company. Good leaders go to extraordinary efforts to determine if a candidate is a match and act quickly when they feel someone is not a fit.	**Hire Slow, Fire Slower** When a good match becomes a misalignment, then try to realign before you let someone go. Great leaders take the time to reconsider the application of an employee's potential before they graduate them.

CLOSING

Your Leadership Lives on for Generations

I have only seen my dad cry once in my entire life. It happened when I was home for the weekend from college. During a typical meal at my parents' kitchen table, I looked out the window. In the distance I could see the grade school I went to as a child. It struck me that my father never told me much about his childhood, minus a camp he went to when he was twelve. So I casually asked him about his family and what his formative years were like.

Suddenly his eyes welled up with tears and he started to cry. All he could mutter was, "I had to be on my knees and hold bricks over my head. I don't know what I did. I don't know what I did." He sobbed so deeply. I had no idea. I never saw my dad cry again. And I never heard another word on what had happened. Or how many times it had happened.

My dad, John P. Michalowicz, was born in the tenements on New York's Lower East Side in 1928. If you don't know about the tenements, they were congested apartment buildings that housed more than fifteen thousand people, mostly dirt-poor immigrants. The conditions for many were deplorable and unlivable, spreading diseases like malaria and the Spanish flu. In its 1902 report, the Tenement House Department stated that "tenement conditions have been found to be so bad as to be indescribable in print."

Even after the Tenement House Act of 1902 forced landlords to improve some conditions, like installing an "operating" toilet in the hallway for each floor, it was rough living for immigrants like my dad's family. And like so many kids he grew up with, my dad faced a fair share of tragedy. His mother, Elizabeth, was put into an asylum when he was five years old, leaving him and his brothers to be raised by their abusive father. (The man with the bricks.)

But this is not a tragic story.

This is also not a story about my dad.

This is a story about a great leader, Helen Fuller.

When my dad became unable to walk in his final year, I would visit him multiple times a week and ask him and my mom questions about their life. Initially, I did this to pass the time. Then I realized it was an opportunity to get my tight-lipped, Greatest Generation parents to open up about their past, to tell me stories I hadn't heard before.

One day I asked, "Who is the person who had the most influence on your life?"

Without hesitation he said, "Helen Fuller." Tears welled up in his eyes. Tears of joy, this time. He smiled ear to ear.

I had never heard the name before, so I pressed him to tell me more. I learned that Mrs. Fuller worked for the Community Service Society (CSS), an organization formed in 1939 with the mission that "every New Yorker deserves to live with dignity and economic security." My dad was one of the first children to benefit from the program.

Mrs. Fuller only met with my dad a few times, but she was more of a parent to him than his father was, or his mother could ever be. They met for the first time when Dad was twelve years old. From his story, it was clear that she had listened deeply to him. That she wanted to learn about his dreams. That she saw his potential and guided him to explore it.

That summer, she sent him to a CSS camp in Maine. My dad called it "Camp Snug-in-the-Woods," but I can't find any record of it. Perhaps it was the name the kids gave it. Whatever name it goes by, that camp helped my dad see another way to live. It gave him a chance to be free from the dangerous conditions he lived in. And it gave him a chance to imagine a future beyond the fate of so many tenement children.

Mrs. Fuller met with my dad at least twice more. She suggested he go to college and explained exactly how to do it. With her support, he joined the military, which helped fund his education. After his military service and college graduation, my dad landed a job, and as was far more common back in those days, worked there his entire life. He worked for Foster Wheeler from the day he completed his schooling to the day he retired. During his tenure he was an engineer, a sales manager, and ultimately a project manager, overseeing the building of oil refineries throughout the globe.

More importantly, Dad lived a good life. He was a loving husband and father. He was gentle, supportive, and kind. When I wanted to learn to play guitar, he paid for my lessons, even though no one in my house was musically inclined. (Ahem . . . including me, which I ultimately discovered.) When I subsequently demonstrated my rendition of AC/DC's "Back in Black" on my out-of-tune guitar that was way too loud and distorted, he smiled at the end and, with my mom, gave me my first ever standing ovation. The only music Dad listened to was concertos by Beethoven, Vivaldi, and Bach, yet he never told me to turn my music down—the volume or my interest. He encouraged me to explore my potential.

When I wanted to play sports, Dad cheered me on, even though no one in the house was an athlete. And when I started my first company, guess who backed me? I had no idea what I was doing. It was risky and crazy. And while neither my parents nor my relatives were entrepreneurs, my parents gave me money from their retirement savings to go for it, without hesitation.

When he handed over the money, Dad patted me on the back and said, "Give 'em all you got. See if it's for you."

My parents also signed up to be the office cleaning crew. Talk about support. Talk about believing in someone who just wants to try. Talk about supporting someone else's potential, especially when it is not yours.

It wasn't until Dad mentioned Mrs. Fuller that I thought about *his* impact on me. Deeply ingrained in me is the belief that everyone is exceptional, and everyone has potential. I see now that it came from my dad. And the reason it came from my dad is because he had the gift of Mrs. Fuller's leadership. She saw potential in him. My dad saw potential in me. I see it in you. Clear as day.

Mrs. Fuller was the definition of great leadership. She saw potential in the children who other people had written off and then nurtured that potential. Because she did that for my dad, he saw the potential in others and nurtured it. I've gone on to do the same. And perhaps my children will be the next potential seers.

Great leadership begets great leadership.

Your leadership will have an impact not just on your team but on the teams they go on to work with, on their children, and on their children's children.

I wonder if you even realize it: you have the greatest potential that exists. You can develop and grow yourself by developing and growing the potential in others. That's a big deal. You are a big deal. Yes, you are a big deal. I do not say that lightly. Great leadership is defined by service, impact, and care for others. It doesn't matter the size of the company you own or work for. It doesn't matter if you work for a business or manage a family. It doesn't matter if you care for hundreds of individuals, or if you are guiding just one other person. Or maybe you are in the throes of life's challenges, and you are simply called to lead yourself. No matter your circumstances, you are a leader. And your opportunity for greatness is in your reach.

Great leadership is not necessarily the famous folks or the big names. Yeah, surely, we could rattle off how great some of those folks are, but I think that would be a disservice to Helen Fuller. I think it would be a disservice to you and the impact you have.

Great leaders guide others to their greatness. You don't have to be famous, or lead a large company, or perform a heroic act that lands you on the six o'clock news. All that's required for great leadership is great caring. And as you already know, that begins with seeing potential in people and taking action to develop it. That is what great leaders do.

You have the opportunity to elevate everyone you touch, even if you only work with them for a year, even if your involvement with them is a single contact. Regardless of the time, I do know this. When you help one person, support one person, change one person's life, they never forget. I bet you can reflect on your own life and quickly identify people who have had great impact on you. I suspect they did because they cared about you and for you. They helped you be more you. They may have even helped you become the person you were meant to be.

You are in the role of a lifetime. You have the chance to help others be more of themselves. And perhaps, just perhaps, that is the kindest gift you can give to all humanity.

In ecology, the "cascade effect" refers to a "sequence of events in which each produces the circumstances necessary for the initiation of the next." It's often used when referencing climate disasters. For example, one small change in nature can affect the entire ecosystem, because each change causes another change, which causes another change, and so on. With humans, the cascade effect can also work in a positive way.

Mrs. Fuller sees potential in my dad, who then starts to see himself differently. He then is a better, more evolved, more hopeful person, and in turn is a better father to me and my sister. Dad sees potential in us, and we both live our lives unafraid to try new things. My sister, too, became an entrepreneur for her first time in her fifties. The first person cheering her on? Dad.

We feel supported in ways our dad was not, and then we transfer that level of support to our children, to our teams, to our social groups. Mrs. Fuller's support for my dad has had a cascading effect that changed countless lives for the better.

Your leadership will also have a cascading effect. It already has, good or bad. Intentional or accidental. But, today, you have an opportunity to make a choice. Will you use your powers for intentional good? Will you use your powers to grow human potential?

Great leaders create *generations of impact*.

In the pages of this book, you have not just learned the value of finding and nurturing your employees' potential, you have discovered a proven path forward. You've learned the formula to create an unstoppable team: fit + ability + safety + ownership (FASO). And you have gained the tools and ideas to apply that formula to your own business.

You've also learned what *doesn't* work, the beliefs, strategies, and systems that have been hampering your business growth and making it difficult for you to recruit and retain top performers who truly care about your business. You can let these outdated and potentially harmful business strategies go, now. You're ready to make your stand.

You now understand if you want your team to be all in for your company, you need to be all in for your team. And now you know exactly how to do that.

And you now understand, FASO goes beyond your business problems and goals.

This is the way you will change the world.

In his final days, my dad lost his ability to speak. The last time I heard him speak, I asked him the same question I'd ask him months before: "Who had the most important influence on your life?" I had forgotten her name, and I wanted to write it down so I could share it with you.

Dad's voice was so weak I couldn't understand his mumbling. So I asked him again. Still, I could not understand.

Then I said, "Dad, can you spell her name?"

"H . . . E . . . L . . . E . . . N," he said. "F . . . U . . . L . . . L . . . E . . . R."

I wrote each letter of her name on my notepad. There she was. My dad's biggest influence, the greatest leader in his life. Helen Fuller. What an honor, to be the person someone remembers in their final breaths.

Great leaders don't make people believe in them. They make people believe in themselves. That is what Helen Fuller did for my father and countless other children who, without her guidance and support, may have never expressed or realized all that was waiting inside to be revealed.

I honor you, Mrs. Fuller.

I miss you, Dad.

Good Leaders	Great Leaders
Go all in.	Are all in.

ACKNOWLEDGMENTS

You know what I discovered when I wrote my first book? It takes a team. My fantasy of feverishly typing away in a cabin near a pond, walking out with literary gold was just that—a fantasy. After a year of effort, in my basement next to the furnace, I had created a literary turd. Then I met the person who would forever transform my life: Anjanette.

Anjanette Harper, you've been turning my raw, uncut ideas into literary gems with each and every book we create. Just when I think it is impossible to raise the bar, you've outdone yourself again. You, my friend, are the definition of artistry and effort. Your friendship means the world to me.

Noah Schwartzberg, nothing makes my day like a call from you saying, "This is your best book ever." And nothing destroys my day more than a call from you saying, "We need a cut here or there." But it is within this delicate push and pull where a book comes to its best form. I am forever indebted to you for questioning and improving the concepts, cutting and expanding the text, and still keeping my voice intact. Hats off to you, my friend!

Danielle Mulvey, the only thing that can match your drive is your love for entrepreneurs, leaders, family, and friends. The ALL IN Company you have created is extraordinary in impact and unmatched in caring. I cherish the times we have spent together touring the country, speaking to entrepreneurs, and deep diving into every business idea imaginable.

And to my unsung heroes working behind the scenes to make the entrepreneurial journey a breeze. Kelsey Ayres, Amy Cartelli, Jenna Lorenz, Andrea Conway, Erin Chazotte, Isabel Capodanno, Adayla Michalowicz, and Cordé Reed—you guys rock! Your dedication and hard work have made this mission possible.

I hope you have found this book to be of great service to you. Honestly, I hope you have fallen in love with it. As you can see, this book is a result of a team effort. An all-in team effort.

P.S. Anjanette, if my calculations are right, we will in fact be putting the finishing touches on the next book while sitting at a pond. A really, really big pond. Thank you for creating my dreams and congratulations on creating yours.

NOTES

INTRODUCTION

ix   **a ballpoint pen:** Will Stewart, "Pictured: Guard Who Ruined £740,000 Painting by Drawing Eyes on It," *Mail Online*, February 11, 2022, dailymail.co.uk/news/article-10502763/Pictured-Bored -security-guard-ruined-740-000-painting-drawing-eyes-it.html. Accessed July 3, 2022.

x   **"I'm very proud of this piece":** "Where Museum Guards Pick the Art," CBS News, March 27, 2022, cbsnews.com/news/baltimore -museum-of-art-guarding-the-art. Accessed July 3, 2022.

CHAPTER 2: ELIMINATE ENTROPY

22   **once in every six thousand or so attempts:** Daniel B. Murray and Scott W. Teare, "Probability of a Tossed Coin Landing on Edge," *Physical Review E* 48, issue 4 (October 1993): 2547–52, journals .aps.org/pre/abstract/10.1103/PhysRevE.48.2547.

CHAPTER 3: RECRUIT POTENTIAL

46 **at a given salary range:** Dana Rodriguez, "A Practical Definition of 'A Player,'" Topgrading, November 22, 2018, topgrading.com /resources/blog/a-practical-definition-of-a-player.

52 **Eddie Van Halen is one of the best:** Jim Farber, "Eddie Van Halen, Virtuoso of the Rock Guitar, Dies at 64," *New York Times*, October 6, 2020, nytimes.com/2020/10/06/arts/music/eddie-van -halen-dead.html. Accessed September 2, 2022.

CHAPTER 5: MAINTAIN A SECURE AND ACCEPTING ENVIRONMENT

91 **the term "unintended consequences":** "Unintended Consequences," Wikipedia, May 30, 2008, en.wikipedia.org/wiki/Unintended _consequences. Accessed November 20, 2022.

91 **violent crimes increased:** Radha Iyengar, "I'd Rather Be Hanged for a Sheep Than a Lamb: The Unintended Consequences of 'Three-Strikes' Laws," NBER, February 7, 2008, nber.org/papers /w13784.

91 **In Australia, a study showed:** Mike Archer, "Ordering the Vegetarian Meal? There's More Animal Blood on Your Hands," *The Conversation*, December 15, 2011, theconversation.com /ordering-the-vegetarian-meal-theres-more-animal-blood-on-your -hands-4659.

92 **"Ghost Girls" was the name:** Kate Moore, "The Forgotten Story of the Radium Girls, Whose Deaths Saved Thousands of Lives," *BuzzFeed*, May 5, 2017, buzzfeed.com/authorkatemoore/the-light -that-does-not-lie. Accessed November 30, 2022.

96 **Project Aristotle:** Charles Duhigg, "What Google Learned from Its Quest to Build the Perfect Team," *New York Times Magazine*, February 25, 2016, nytimes.com/2016/02/28/magazine/what-google

-learned-from-its-quest-to-build-the-perfect-team.html. Accessed December 4, 2022.

CHAPTER 6: FOSTER PSYCHOLOGICAL OWNERSHIP

98   **This supports research around:** Bill Fotsch and John Case, "The Business Case for Open-Book Management," *Forbes,* July 25, 2017, forbes.com/sites/fotschcase/2017/07/25/the-business-case-for -open-book-management. Accessed April 14, 2023.

105   **"Everyone here has a custodial relationship":** Patricia Corrigan, "Baltimore Museum Security Staff Curate a Show of Their Own," Next Avenue, April 29, 2022, nextavenue.org/museum-security -staff-members-curate-a-show-of-their-favorite-art. Accessed December 26, 2022.

106   **"Not at all familiar":** "Jon L. Pierce," The Science of Ownership, October 8, 2014, thescienceofownership.org/facesvoices/featured /jon-l-pierce.

107   **Pierce, Rubenfeld, and Morgan published an article:** Jon L. Pierce, Stephen A. Rubenfeld, and Susan Morgan, "Employee Ownership: A Conceptual Model of Process and Effects," *Academy of Management Review* 16, no. 1 (January 1991): 121–44, jstor.org /stable/258609. Accessed December 26, 2022.

CHAPTER 10: UP-LEVEL EMPLOYEE EXPERIENCE AND PERFORMANCE

183   **A study conducted by Umeå University:** Tracy Brower, "Learning Is a Sure Path to Happiness: Science Proves It," *Forbes,* October 17, 2021, forbes.com/sites/tracybrower/2021/10/17/learning-is-a-sure -path-to-happiness-science-proves-it. Accessed November 23, 2022.

184 **94 percent of employees:** Abigail Johnson Hess, "LinkedIn: 94% of Employees Say They Would Stay at a Company Longer for This Reason—And It's Not a Raise," CNBC, February 27, 2019, cnbc.com/2019/02/27/94percent-of-employees-would-stay-at-a-company-for-this-one-reason.html. Accessed November 21, 2022.

189 **Gary Chapman and Paul White's:** Karl Moore, "The 5 Languages of Appreciation at Work," *Forbes*, April 18, 2022, forbes.com/sites/karlmoore/2022/04/18/the-five-languages-of-appreciation-at-work. Accessed November 20 2022.

194 **On a strength-to-density ratio:** "Strong Like Spider Silk," *Science*, November 20, 2018, science.org/content/article/spider-silk-five-times-stronger-steel-now-scientists-know-why. Accessed December 30, 2022.

196 **In his TED Talk:** Tom Wujec, "Build a Tower, Build a Team," TED Talk, ted.com/talks/tom_wujec_build_a_tower_build_a_team. Accessed November 20, 2022.

196 **United Nations' Least Developed Country:** United Nations, "Least Developed Country Category: Bhutan Profile," un.org/development/desa/dpad/least-developed-country-category-bhutan.html. Accessed November 20, 2022.

197 **Oxford Poverty and Human Development Initiative:** Oxford Poverty and Human Development Initiative, "Bhutan's Gross National Happiness Index," ophi.org.uk/policy/gross-national-happiness-index. Accessed November 20, 2022.

197 **World Economic Forum's article:** Lyonpo Loknath Sharma and Ratnakar Adhikari, "What Bhutan Got Right About Happiness—and What Other Countries Can Learn," World Economic Forum, weforum.org/agenda/2021/10/lessons-from-bhutan-economic-development. Accessed November 20, 2002.

CHAPTER 11: ADAPT TO CHANGING WORK ENVIRONMENTS

201 **get your ass in the office:** Kim Bhasin, "Best Buy CEO: Here's Why I Killed the 'Results Only Work Environment,'" *Business Insider*, March 18, 2013, businessinsider.com/best-buy-ceo-rowe-2013-3. Accessed November 18, 2022.

201 **"fundamentally flawed":** Seth Stevenson, "Would You Do Your Job Better If Your Boss Didn't Care How You Did It?," *Slate*, May 12, 2014, slate.com/business/2014/05/best-buys-rowe-experiment-can -results-only-work-environments-actually-be-successful.html. Accessed November 18, 2022.

202 **an outlier year of 2021:** "Revenue for Best Buy (BBY)," CompaniesMarketCap.com, companiesmarketcap.com/best-buy /revenue. Accessed November 18, 2022.

204 **US surgeon general Vivek Murthy:** Vivek Murthy, "Work and the Loneliness Epidemic," *Harvard Business Review*, September 26, 2017, hbr.org/2017/09/work-and-the-loneliness-epidemic.

205 **In a conversation with a *Bloomberg* journalist:** Justin Fox, "Are Workers More Productive at Home?" *Bloomberg*, June 2, 2022, bloomberg.com/opinion/articles/2022-06-02/are-workers-more -productive-at-home.

208 **simple screening, treatment, and education:** Paul Hemp, "Presentee-ism: At Work—But Out of It," *Harvard Business Review*, October 1, 2004, hbr.org/2004/10/presenteeism-at-work-but-out-of-it.

208 **never missed a day of work:** Allie Gold, "Man Goes Viral for Never Missing a Day of Work in 27 Years," Q104.3, June 28, 2022, q1043 .iheart.com/content/2022-06-28-man-goes-viral-for-never -missing-a-day-of-work-in-27-years.

208 **"I would love to have a day off":** Ieva Gailiūtė and Mindaugas Balčiauskas, "'They've Kind of Lost Touch with Their Workers':

Man Shows a 'Goodie Bag' He Received from Burger King to Celebrate 27 Years of Loyalty," *Bored Panda*, boredpanda.com /burger-king-employee-27-years-perfect-attendance-goodie-bag. Accessed December 30, 2022.

CHAPTER 12: LET PEOPLE GO

221 **rather than the parts:** "Gestalt Psychology," Psych Web, psywww .com/intropsych/ch04-senses/gestalt-psychology.html. Accessed November 19, 2022.

221 **Gestalt Language Protocol:** Subhanjan Sarkar, "The Gestalt (Language) Protocol," Pitch.Link, June 24, 2019, pitch.link/blog /the-gestalt-language-protocol.

225 **advice from marriage and family therapist:** Sarah Regan, "How to Actually Let Go of Someone & 14 Signs It's Time, from Therapists," *MindBodyGreen*, April 14, 2022, mindbodygreen.com/articles /how-to-let-go-of-someone. Accessed November 19, 2022.

231 **organizational psychologist Tasha Eurich:** Tasha Eurich, "Increase Your Self-Awareness with One Simple Fix," TED Talk, ted.com /talks/tasha_eurich_increase_your_self_awareness_with_one _simple_fix. Accessed November 19, 2022.

CLOSING: YOUR LEADERSHIP LIVES ON FOR GENERATIONS

236 **"as to be indescribable in print":** Stuart Marques, "The Early Tenements of New York—Dark, Dank, and Dangerous," NYC Department of Records & Information Services, May 17, 2019, archives.nyc/blog/2019/5/16/the-early-tenements-of-new-yorkdark -dank-and-dangerous.

240 **"cascade effect" refers:** Oxford Reference, oxfordreference.com /display/10.1093/oi/authority.20110803095552857. Accessed November 12, 2022.

INDEX

Page numbers in italics indicate tables and charts.

BUILD YOUR
UNSTOPPABLE TEAM

☑ Easily recruit the best candidates

☑ Have everyone act like an owner

☑ Retain your best people forever

☑ Raise the bar for your entire organization

Free resources and tools to build an unstoppable team!

Priority access to workshops and training sessions!

Ensure you do *ALL IN* the right way!

Download the free resources and join our workshop at

AllinByMike.com

Read more from Mike Michalowicz